Working on
BULLEID PACIFICS

By Derek Phillips

Rebuilt 34010 SIDMOUTH at Chichester with the 11am Brighton to Plymouth on 28 March 1964.
Lens of Sutton Association.

Irwell Press Ltd.

Acknowledgements

Preparing a book such as this would not be possible without the assistance of many people with working memories, information, photographs, encouragement, and support. I am very grateful to former railwaymen who contributed memories of their working days on the Bulleid Pacifics: Jim Lester of Nine Elms, Bob Cartwright of Eastleigh, Nigel Vidaurri of Nine Elms, Fred Butler, Roy Turner, Gordon Pearson, Mike Mullarkey from Exmouth Junction, Gerald Smallabrooke from Okehampton and my old friend and fellow fireman from Yeovil Town shed Dave Brown. I have also included a memoir from the late Arthur Turner. The South Western Circle have kindly allowed me to use the John Eyers collection, Mike King the A.E. West collection. I have also to thank Tony Sheffield of RailOnline, Robin and Sarah Fell from Transport Treasury, Peter Fidczuk and Terry Walsh from the Lens of Sutton Association, Peter and Heather Foster for their research on working timetables and Southern Locomotives Ltd.

Further Reading

Practical Hints for Footplate Men. Southern Railway. Traffic Department. Motive Power.
Locomotives of the Southern Railway Part 2. D.L. Bradley. RCTS.
The Book of the West Country and Battle of Britain Pacifics. Richard Derry. Irwell Press.
The Book of the Merchant Navy Pacifics. Richard Derry, Ian Sixsmith. Irwell Press.
An Historical Survey of Southern Sheds. Chris Hawkins & George Reeve. Irwell Press.
Bulleid Power The Merchant Navy Class. A.J. Fry. Alan Sutton Publishing Ltd.
Southern Steam Surrender. John H. Bird. Kingfisher Railway Productions.
Southern Region Engine Workings. C.J. Gammell. Oxford Publishing Co.
Somerset & Dorset Locomotive History. D. Bradley, David Milton. David & Charles.

First published in the United Kingdom in 2022,
by Irwell Press Limited, 59A, High Street, Clophill,
Bedfordshire MK45 4BE
Tel: 01525 861888
www.irwellpress.com

Contents

CHANNEL PACKET under preparation at Salisbury shed (note fireman getting his coal in order) on 26 September 1946. Five years on, it is not quite the striking 1941 original shown opposite, following a number of alterations in the light of experience. Small smoke deflectors have been fitted, the smokebox door plate is now a full roundel, there are now three sandbox filler apertures serving all of the coupled wheels compared to the previous single aperture; the 'widow's peak' had been replaced by a smokebox hood in December 1943. The livery is now full malachite green, applied in November 1945. Standard smoke deflectors were attached in August 1947. R.C. Riley, transporttreasury

Salisbury's 21C9 SHAW SAVILL adorned with the DEVON BELLE 'wings' takes water at Exmouth Junction on 3 July 1948; its malachite green livery was changed to BR blue in August 1949. Lens of Sutton Association.

Introduction

Allocated new to Salisbury in June 1941, the pioneer Merchant Navy with its distinctive 'widow's peak' cowling is in the shed yard at Exmouth Junction a little later in the year. 21C1 CHANNEL PACKET is in matt malachite green livery with three yellow horizontal lines. The gun metal 'inverted horseshoe' SOUTHERN plate on the smokebox door was replaced by a full roundel after numerous complaints that a horseshoe so disposed was unlucky. You'd never see one so displayed on a ship for instance, and this was the Merchant Navy class, after all... Fitted with steam sanding, only one centrally placed sand filler aperture is provided with a single pipe serving the front of the middle driving wheel only. The sand filler aperture is just forward of the nameplate; initially the first five locomotives were so equipped. This arrangement proved inadequate and additional sand boxes were fitted for the leading and trailing coupled wheels. The second and third series of locomotives were also equipped with steam sanding to all coupled wheels, plus hand operated sanding to the front tender wheels. The sand boxes for the leading driving wheels were later removed with the filler aperture blanked off. Sanding for the leading coupled wheels was reinstated when the locomotives were rebuilt. 21C1 has gun metal plates on the tender, cab sides and above the buffer beam. The photograph was taken in August 1941 when the front numberplate was moved from the sloping section of sheeting and repositioned lower down on the vertical sheeting, the electric marker lights and disc brackets were then moved above to the sloping section. Lens of Sutton Association.

I was born during the dark days of the Second World War in 1941. My entry into the world, although a happy event for my lovely mum and dad, did not meet however with quite the same incredulity that attended the appearance of the first Merchant Navy in the same year. It would be fair to say that British locomotive building, in the forefront of innovation, advancement, and design of the finest steam locomotives since the days of George Stephenson, was taken aback upon the coming of the pioneer 21C1 with its air-smooth casing which encompassed the smokebox, boiler and cab. To some, it looked as if it may have arrived from outer space.

Appearances aside, this was a revolutionary design reflecting the brilliance of its creator. The first steam locomotive in Great Britain to be equipped with electric lighting powered by a steam driven generator, the first Pacific to run on the Southern Railway. The ground-breaking features have been recounted in so many publications: oil-bath enclosed valve gear, wide Belpaire firebox and inner all-welded steel box, BFB wheels, thermic syphons, 280lb/sq.in. working pressure, electric lighting, Lemaitre blastpipe and air-smooth casing. Another innovation was the (partial) rocker grate which was a boon for the firemen of the Southern Railway used to throwing clinker from the side of the cab on the older classes of engines. Bulleid's unique numbering scheme too, confounded observers. 21C1. The 2 denotes the number of leading bogie axles, 1 the trailing bogie axles, C = three coupled axles. 1: Engine number.

Thirty of the Merchant Navy class were built in three batches of ten. The smaller West Country/Battle of Britain classes appeared from 1945. 110 came to be built by the Southern Railway and British Railways after it. The thirty Merchant Navys, and sixty light Pacifics, were rebuilt turning them into a stunning looking locomotive – for a second time! I feel profoundly honoured to have had the privilege of working on these magnificent machines along the switchback route of the Salisbury to Exeter main line back in the day when I was a young fireman at Yeovil Town engine shed and I still remember to this day my first ever firing trip on a West Country working a stopping passenger train along the main line from Exeter Central to Yeovil Junction under the eagle eye of Senior Locomotive Inspector Sam Smith.

This was the feared 'passed cleaners firing test', which I passed although it was nerve racking at the time. This led to promotion to fireman in due course working on the classes on the line at the time including S15 and King Arthur 4-6-0s, U class 2-6-0s, BR class 4MT 2-6-0s and 5MT 4-6-0s, all fine locomotives with a few rough trips thrown in. For me, the top of the tree and the 'Rolls Royce' of locomotives were the Bulleid Pacifics which were unequalled in my firing experiences.

I have fired the locomotives in their original and rebuilt versions and never had a problem for the steaming qualities of the boiler were excellent. They had to be fired correctly, mind; keeping the back corners stacked full on a Bulleid was vital. The cabs were also the best, relatively draught free and comfortable, the padded seats a boon compared to the wooden flaps of other engines. Electric power courtesy of a Stones steam driven generator was an excellent attribute, it meant no more headlamps and gauge lamps to refill and light, except one used as a tail lamp. A full set of headlamps was carried just in case the generator packed up, and it did fail with me on a couple of occasions. The engines in their original condition were well known for their slipping, although I had certain drivers who could manage them with practised ease with never a hint of losing their feet.

Dear reader, I do hope you enjoy the working memories and the photographs of Bulleid Pacifics at work on the Southern Railway and the Southern Region of British Railways; we shall never see the like again. As young men in our prime, we worked on these legendary locomotives many years ago in all winds and weather fair or foul, day or night on passenger or goods trains. Unfortunately we are now getting very thin on the ground as the years advance, however our memories of those days of the locomotives and our comrades that we once worked with will never diminish.

Derek Phillips
Somerset

Below. Nine Elms' 21C14 NEDERLAND LINE ready to depart from Waterloo on the Devon Belle about 1948. The striking SOUTHERN RAILWAY roundel also has the building year EASTLEIGH 1945. 21C14, in malachite green, never acquired BR blue. Lens of Sutton Association.

Right. 21C120 SEATON arriving at Salisbury with the 8.15am from Plymouth on 21 September 1946.

Bottom right. Newly outshopped from Eastleigh Works on 29 June 1957, the first light Pacific to be rebuilt, 34005 BARNSTAPLE absolutely immaculate at Eastleigh station on 9 July 1957 with the 5.16pm Portsmouth to Basingstoke. The locomotive had been stopped at Nine Elms with badly fractured frames and a damaged middle cylinder, so was an ideal candidate for modification. It had to be towed from Nine Elms to Eastleigh for the rebuilding. 34005 was also attached at the time of rebuilding to tender 3358 which had previously been with 34094 MORTEHOE. *The Railway Observer* noted that it worked from Eastleigh at first, and that its maiden passenger duty was to Bournemouth and back on 4 July. In mid-August it went to Stewarts Lane where its first working was a boat train. The authorities obviously wanted to ascertain its capabilities, and they weren't disappointed. Which was just as well, for while BARNSTAPLE was going through its paces, 34027 TAW VALLEY was already undergoing rebuilding at Eastleigh. L.R. Freeman, transporttreasury.

Nine Elms fireman Nigel Vidaurri removing the tail lamp from 35013 BLUE FUNNEL at Waterloo before working a Sunday service to Bournemouth. Nigel is an old friend of mine as we were both engine cleaners and firemen at Yeovil Town MPD until he later transferred to Nine Elms. Courtesy Nigel Vidaurri.

Driver Jim Evans and fireman Nigel Vidaurri were working the 7.24am Bournemouth Central to Waterloo on 28 October 1965 with 35004 CUNARD WHITE STAR when the locomotive suffered a severe wheel slip near Hook resulting in broken and buckled coupling rods, rendering the engine a complete failure. Nigel is seen here posing with the buckled rods. This would have been an easy repair for Eastleigh Works, but under BR policy by then, repairs were not authorised, and the locomotive was withdrawn. A.J. Fry (*Bulleid Power The Merchant Navy Class*, Sutton Publishing) notes that 35004 was cut up at Eastleigh shed in February 1966 by Cohen's. Courtesy Nigel Vidaurri.

Jim Lester, Nine Elms

During the late 1950s and early 1960s, the 'Bournemouth Belle' was worked by Bournemouth depot during the weekdays but it was always a Nine Elms duty at the weekends. The introduction of the 'Royal Wessex' in 1951 in association with the Festival of Britain had seen the weekday 'Belle' transferred to Bournemouth while Nine Elms crews worked the new train in both directions. The Nine Elms Top Link nevertheless still had the 'Belle' on Saturdays and No.2 Link or 'Pilot Gang' as it was generally known, would work it on Sundays. In terms of who actually worked the train there was no question of any particular crew being selected; it was determined solely by roster rotation and when it was your turn, that was it!

I have a few memories of the 'Belle' the first being rather an odd one. On this particular occasion, having relieved the Nine Elms preparation crew at the top of No.11 platform at Waterloo we were issued with a special 'stop order' by the Guard to call at Beaulieu Road station, a small country station in the middle of the

New Forest. Apparently, as it turned out, to allow Lord Montague to alight there, it being his local station! The order was quite explicit in that the driver should ensure that the third coach from the front was stopped so as to give access to the platform. When you've had a railway running across your land since the 1850s it is interesting what preferential treatment you could still demand!

It was practice at that time, rather quaintly, to give both the driver and fireman of the 'Belle' a bottle of light ale when the train stopped at Southampton Central. One of the Pullman stewards would come walking down the platform with a tray with two bottles on it and we would consume them with relish! God bless George Mortimer Pullman, is what I say, or said. Of course, by today's standards, this would not be allowed but the railway was quite different in those days, and it is quite amusing looking back on it!

I had worked the 'Belle' on a number of occasions and most of these were routine trips. However, my driver, Bill Turner and I were faced with a bit of a problem when

we were in charge of the up train on the 17 March 1963. In the morning, we had worked the 11.30am down from Waterloo to Bournemouth West, stopping at Basingstoke, Winchester and numerous other stations on the way down. We arrived at Bournemouth West at 2.20pm and then, after being shunt released, ran light to Bournemouth Central and left our locomotive, a Standard Class 5, 73081 EXCALIBUR, on the pit in the depot for servicing. I recorded that on the down trip the engine was not steaming freely, possibly due to the poor quality coal. After a meal break, we took charge of 35030 ELDER DEMPSTER LINES, a Nine Elms Merchant Navy that I knew to be a good one. We departed the depot at 3.55pm and ran tender first to Bournemouth West to collect the up 'Belle' which left at 4.30pm.

The first part of our journey was uneventful as we made our way towards London and after stopping and taking water at Southampton Central, we continued the second leg of the trip making good time climbing the bank and passing Basingstoke with time to spare. In those days, the coming into contact with the top of the conductor rail. The knock-on effect was that as it short-circuited the energised rail it was also blowing out the circuit breaker in the Electrical Control depriving the section of line immediately ahead and behind us of power! The Electrical Power Controller at Woking would have been aware of the situation immediately and would have put the breaker back a couple of times in an attempt to restore the power. He was not allowed to do this more than twice, until the cause was identified and the correct remedial action determined.

We therefore knew that we were going to be stopped even as we passed through Woking with green signals at about 80mph. Sure enough on approaching West Byfleet, the semaphore distant was 'on'. We had been running well and in good time, but knew we would not be allowed to continue while all this was happening. West Byfleet's home signal was at danger as we approached and we slowed right down; the signal cleared very slowly indicating that observation from the signal box was required. Pulling slowly forward we stopped opposite the signal box where the signalman, now standing at the box window, could see what we were doing. We indicated to him that we understood the problem and after checking the Up Local was clear, I climbed down on to the track, armed with the ashpan 'rocker bar'. With this the door could be yanked back in place for the catch to be banged in behind it. The signalman witnessed exactly what was happening and just as I had finished, he was clearing his signals. Back on the footplate Bill was already setting the train in motion as I climbed onboard to join him. Getting away from West Byfleet was not too difficult with the gradient slightly in our favour, even with our train of eleven Pullman coaches. Bill then extended 35030, as he often had on other occasions to regain time; she responded well and we still managed to arrive at Waterloo 'right time'.

Fred Butler, Exmouth Junction

We were working the up Atlantic Coast Express late in 1954, ACE 12.30 Exeter Central to Waterloo with 35023 HOLLAND-AFRIKA LINE, doing well for timing and speed. As we neared the Broad Clyst distant signal, the tender started jumping and banging alarmingly. Driver Pooley immediately got the train under

Nigel Vidaurri looks back from the cab of an unrebuilt Pacific approaching Waterloo; in the distance a rebuilt engine awaiting departure lifts its safety valves. Courtesy Nigel Vidaurri.

first electrified conductor rail encountered was on the Up Local where the line from Ascot was linked to the main line at Sturt Lane Junction having come off the single line to Ash Vale at Frimley Junction. A few miles further on at Pirbright Junction saw the line from Alton similarly join the Up Local. Then, as you passed through Brookwood station, there was a crossover from the electrified Up Local to the Up Through line and from that point onwards there was a continuous conductor rail on both lines leading into Waterloo. Locomotives generally rode

somewhat rougher over electrified lines due, it was said, to the effect that electric units had on the permanent way, and this became quite noticeable once running over these lines. On this day as we passed through Brookwood at quite high speed might I add, there was a loud bang from underneath the engine. Bill looked at me with a puzzled expression and then, a little later, there was another similar bang. It was then we realised what had happened; the ashpan hopper door, normally held in place by a locking catch, had somehow fallen open and now was control, closing the regulator and stopping at the signal box. Climbing down from the footplate to see what was wrong, we discovered that the leading tender axle had snapped and knocked an alarmingly large hole in the bottom of the tender – through which we were losing all the water. I had to chuck the fire out and by luck had the help of Jack Hobbs, a Salisbury fireman who happened to be going home passenger. This was no easy task on the main line; the box was full of fire and the coal incandescent, and it all had to be pitched out from the cab with the ever-unwieldy clinker shovel. As 35023 quietened down, amid the chaos we were rescued by an engine off the following train and taken to Pinhoe to be put out of the way while everything was sorted out. Another Merchant Navy was conjured up from Exmouth Junction to take the much delayed train forward to Waterloo.

The next time I was on 35023 we had the up Devon Belle on its last day the same year, 1954. We were to work the train to Wilton where the famous engine changeover took place; the fresh engine continued with the train to Waterloo with our relieved engine following on light for disposal at Salisbury MPD. It was not to be on this occasion. Approaching Semley, 35023 suffered a broken valve; we managed to reach the station to come to a stop and the changeover engine waiting at Wilton was sent out to take the train on to Waterloo. A spare was thus ready and waiting, as it were. We followed, limping along to Salisbury MPD; 35023 was certainly not my lucky MN!

Working on the Atlantic Coast Express one day we went through Yeovil Junction at 105mph; that said, another driver once hurtled through Axminster at 108mph. One time, we ran from Salisbury to Sidmouth Junction with the ACE – 75 miles – in 63 minutes. The very next day, driver Bob 'Cowboy' Clements and fireman Bill Smudge ran from Salisbury to Sidmouth Junction in 62 minutes. I don't think anyone from Exmouth Junction ever beat that.

Gordon Pearson, Exmouth Junction
I left National Service in the Army in 1957. I had an interview with Mr Horace Moore the shed master at Exmouth Junction and began working as an engine cleaner in September of that year. I then progressed through the ranks to passed cleaner and fireman. I worked

on trains to Salisbury, Barnstaple Junction, Ilfracombe, Okehampton, Meldon Quarry and Plymouth. My favourite locomotives were the West Countrys and Battle of Britains, the light Pacifics. I was not too keen on the T9s or S15s which seemed obsolete by comparison. I enjoyed my working life at Exmouth Junction where there were over 100 sets of enginemen, many of them good mates of mine.

I remember a trip one Sunday with driver Reg Pridham; we were booked to work a civil engineer's train consisting of lengths of continuous welded track from Exeter to Plymouth Friary via Okehampton and return home light engine. We had one of our excellent West Countrys which as usual steamed well on the journey to Plymouth.

After putting our train away in the sidings at Friary we ran to the engine shed, anticipating a quick and easy run home unencumbered by any load. The foreman had other plans; there had been an engine failure and Control had ordered him to conjure up a spare for a holiday special from Plymouth North Road as far as Exeter St. David's where a Western engine would take the train onwards. We were collared for the job and set off for North Road station where our train of only seven coaches was waiting; we duly coupled up, the guard gave us the load, took my driver's name and the engine number and we were ready to go. We were running back to Exeter on the Western Region main line, so had a pilotman as neither my mate nor I had worked over this line before. Somewhere along the route and I am unable to remember where – Dainton it might have been – the pilotman warned my driver to slow down and stop for a banking engine to assist us on the incline. Reg would have none of it; we didn't slow down and he made the reason plain to the startled pilotman: 'we'll keep on going – we've got a West Country and only seven coaches on'. We passed the banker in its siding and just sailed by. The engine performed superbly under the capable handling of Reg and steamed well. Thinking back, we had two stops, Totnes and Newton Abbot before we eventually arrived at St. David's where a Western engine was waiting to take over. After uncoupling we ran up the bank, back to home ground and on to Exmouth Junction shed where we left the engine on the disposal pit and booked off duty.

Mike Mullarkey, Exmouth Junction
I started work as an apprentice fitter at Exmouth Junction workshops in 1945. This was a six-year apprenticeship with the last year spent at the Locomotive Works at Eastleigh. It was great experience, working on all types of locomotives, but my favourites were the Bulleid Pacifics. I spent a lot of time at Exmouth Junction with a fitter called Jim Mares on what we called the 'Periodical Gang'. This involved major work on the locomotives after a high mileage had been accumulated. It meant stripping down pistons and valves for cleaning and re-ringing new bushes on connecting rods and so on. All springs were renewed, and the upshot was that we had a trip on the footplate, armed with our large spanners, to the GWR depot at Newton Abbot where we could adjust the tension of the springs on the weighbridge there.

I have pleasant memories of overhauling Battle of Britain 34051. This was WINSTON CHURCHILL of course and when he was taken ill it was discreetly decided that, should he pass away, the locomotive would pull the train in which his body would be borne. I did the work with another fitter, Reg Lang but as it turned out Winston happily recovered, but we did get an engine in tip-top condition! The plan obviously remained in place, however, and by the time the Great Man eventually passed away, 34051 had been transferred to Nine Elms. But I still fondly and proudly remember that I did a job for Winston.

Another time I recall the breakdown gang being called out late one night to a derailment, not on the main line but in a siding at Chard or perhaps Crewkerne – it was a long time ago, after all. I cannot remember which, but think it was Chard Junction. Anyway, it was New Years Eve and the derailment had left a Bulleid Pacific at an awkward angle, requiring removal of the tender. Unfortunately we could not release the drawbar pin, so I had to cut through the drawbar with an oxyacetylene torch. This involved lying awkwardly on the trackwork underneath the engine to cut the drawbar, and just before I'd finished, I felt a tug on my leg, with someone shouting 'Happy New Year'. What a way to see it in! Talking of New Year I remember, when working night shifts at Exmouth Junction, just before midnight, everyone would find a locomotive in steam, and at

Balancing precariously on the tender of 34015 EXMOUTH while working a Waterloo-Weymouth service at Southampton Central, Nigel Vidaurri is deftly trying to move some larger lumps of coal down to the shovelling plate. I have done this many times as a young fireman; the knack on the Bulleids was to get a small avalanche of coal down to the shovelling plate. All cleaners and young firemen were 'daredevils' in this regard, myself included. Tricks in the shed on an engine out of steam, included walking along the top of a boiler, hiding in fireboxes, swimming in the depot water tank, and much more…. The Health and Safety would have an apoplexy. Courtesy Nigel Vidaurri.

the stroke of midnight we would all blow their whistles to welcome in the New Year.

I was also part of the snowplough gang and with a fitter's mate and some tools we set off once to the far side of Okehampton where it was snowing badly. The reason for a fitter to accompany the driver and fireman was that the plough had to be lifted to cross the Meldon Viaduct. This meant adjustments using spanners, and the trade unions being like they were in those days, this was deemed a fitter's job, ridiculous really. Anyway, after lots of ploughing through the snow we realised that it was pointless, for it was drifting such to immediately fill in the cleared line behind us. We were not going to get the main line to Plymouth open. Alarmingly, we could not get back either. The amount of snow blowing off Dartmoor was amazing. We were in a siding and thankfully there was a guard's van there, and inside was a stove to keep us warm, so that is where we spent the night. There was a signal box nearby and I managed to get a message to the depot to say that we were stuck and could our families be informed? An engine cleaner was

sent to my home and handed my wife a piece of paper baldly stating: 'Fitter Mullarkey is stuck in a snow drift' – it can be readily imagined that it hardly did much to quieten any fears she had! Eventually, the following day, we made our weary way back – on foot! to Okehampton station and were told an engine would be there later to pick us up. A light Pacific duly turned up and, gratefully ensconced in its warm cab, we were soon back at Exmouth Junction. The good part of the whole experience was that we were being paid overtime for what was almost two days, and this extra money on top of my pay, went towards buying a chest freezer, then an exotic and expensive domestic appliance – don't forget, this was a time when even toasters and electric kettles were far from universal items in the average kitchen. Along with washing machines you were more likely to see them in an American film.

I thoroughly enjoyed my 22 years on the railway working with many friends and workmates and it was a sad day for us all when the depot shut down. Unexpectedly some of the lines that closed in the period have now

reopened. A supermarket has since been built on the site of the engine sheds and workshops at Exmouth Junction. And every time I walk up and down the aisles I almost have to pinch myself: 'I used to work here.'

Roy Turner, Exmouth Junction

I began work on the Southern Railway as an engine cleaner at Exmouth Junction in 1945, later becoming a fireman. I found the original Merchant Navy engines to be extremely free-steaming but as they were not equipped at first with dampers, it was a job to keep them quiet as the safety valves would soon lift. The rebuilt engines, including the light Pacifics, were equipped with dampers, which were better to keep them quiet. When I was in the 'Spare Gang', we'd lodge away at Lyme Regis, Seaton and Bude for about three days at a time in the summer and the quarters were less than salubrious. It was also hard work; only tank engines were allocated but they were coaled in ancient, unchanging fashion, by shovel from a coal wagon parked alongside. A daily diet of fish and chips was one saving grace at least.

So it was always good to get back to Exmouth Junction and the main line. I recall my last trip on the down Atlantic Coast Express; I have in mind the engine was 35025 BROCKLEBANK LINE and a very good one it was at the time. We entered Honiton Tunnel at 50mph, which is impressive especially after climbing the eight miles from Seaton Junction at a grade of 1 in 80. The tunnel at 1,345 yards is the longest on the Southern Region. Cinders and ash would bounce down from the roof, the exhaust would be deafening, with the fierce orange glow from the firebox reflecting around the cab. Approximately half-way through, the gradient decreases, the blast from the chimney grows softer and we increase speed, my mate keeps the regulator open and winds back the reverser, as we accelerate from the west end of the tunnel heading towards our first scheduled stop since leaving Salisbury, at Sidmouth Junction. We had senior Locomotive Inspector Sam Smith riding on the footplate with us that day, and as usual, he would occupy the fireman's seat, as I had plenty to get on with – working a train like the ACE never gave a fireman much time to sit down. I found Sam Smith to be completely fair; if he saw that a fireman was doing his job properly, then there would not be a problem.

When the light Pacifics were new they were fitted with three safety valves positioned ahead of the dome. Water would surge forward in the boiler when braking, to be ejected through the safety valves and this led to many complaints from stations and passengers. Lifting safety valves had also 'drowned' cars waiting at the level crossings, and I think there were lots of complaints from motorists regarding damaged paintwork. The safety valves were eventually reduced to two and repositioned further back along the boiler. At the age of 91 I think back to my firing days on the railway, and still meet some of my old comrades, although we are getting very thin on the ground these days.

Bob Cartwright, Eastleigh
In recent years, many visitors to the Mid Hants 'War on the Line' events have been treated to the wonderful sight and sound of a Supermarine Spitfire in the skies over our railway. My own interest in these iconic machines came about when, as an engine cleaner and fireman at Eastleigh in the early 1960s I often saw

the blue spitfire T9 two-seater trainer 'R.J. Mitchell' which was based at what was then Eastleigh Airport. The aircraft would often pass over the shed when taking off or landing. Like many others, I often dreamed of a flight in a Spit. The nearest I ever got, indeed will ever get, was the locomotive of the same name, 34066 SPITFIRE. Just four weeks or so before she was withdrawn in September 1966, I was fortunate enough to work to London and back with her. Her only somewhat dubious claim to fame was that she was involved in the terrible crash at Lewisham in 1957.

On Saturday 13 August 1966 I was booked to work with Driver Jack Morey on 134 duty, and 34066 was shown to be prepared for us. At this time, the Bournemouth electrification was in its final stages and at weekends, trains would often be diverted, many of them over the Mid Hants, to allow for the long permanent way possessions necessary to complete the work. Our altered diagram would have us work a parcel and mails train to Waterloo, take the engine to Nine Elms depot and carry out requirements (water, coal and fire cleaning). We would then go light engine to Waterloo to work the 03:15 newspaper train back as far as Eastleigh via Alton.

As always there was overtime on offer due to shortages of men and machines and because I arrived at the shed so early, in order to make sure our loco was prepared properly, I was asked to sign on early to 'do requirements' on the standby engine or 'pilot' as we knew them. This was Class 5 73117 VIVIEN. The up and down pilot engines were kept in a twenty-four hour state of readiness in case of failure on the main line and could generally be off shed in around 15 to 20 minutes of a summons being received. While the shed steam raisers would keep their fires alight and boilers filled, they needed to be coaled, watered and generally tidied up at least once every twenty-four hours. It was also not unknown for them to be raided for tools and lamps by late running firemen desperate to save time when preparing their own engines.

Officially, one of the pit gang or 'shed' drivers should have accompanied me from the front of the shed to the disposal pit and coal stage but, as it was Saturday, with no management about, after pushing the fire over and raising a bit more puff I took the loco over to the disposal pit. I dropped most of the accumulated

ash from the grate, took water, then coal, and moved down to the pointsmans hut at the south end of the shed yard. A quick word with Bert the pointsman and it was down over the bottom set of points whilst he set the points for No.8, the through road in the shed, then it was up over the top set of points and back into No.15 road. Push the fire under the brick arch, fill the boiler and 50 minutes after climbing on 73117 she was back in position, refreshed and all ready to go.

Back in the lobby Jack had arrived for our booked turn and on hearing what I had just done made some light-hearted comment like "You'll never live to spend it all, nipper". I left him the tea can and went over the yard to where SPITFIRE was waiting, supposedly ready prepared. I still had some twenty minutes to tidy up and have a wash round the cab before we were due off shed. In those days it was a bit of a lottery as to who got your loco ready and how well they did it so if you wanted a reasonable start it paid to get to the engine early on.

At the appointed time we moved off shed to the exit dummy and I 'rang out' on the rotary train describer to Eastleigh West box. The exit dummy cleared, and we ran through the up platform to wait behind a dummy on the up local for our train to arrive in the platform and the engine to come off. My record of the journey to Waterloo shows that we left Eastleigh at 20:10 with 18 vans equal to a load of 420 tons. On arrival at Waterloo, I uncoupled the engine from the train, and we waited to assist the engine taking the stock to Clapham yard out of the platform.

It is interesting to note with regard to the uncoupling of the engine how this was done when compared to the way that we do it today on the Mid Hants Railway. On closely approaching the stopping point, six feet from the stop blocks, the fireman would step off of the still moving loco at a point where he knew the tender/front coach coupling would stop. As soon as the train stopped moving, he would jump down in between, uncouple the vacuum and steam heat pipes, and place the engine vacuum pipe on its dummy. In the meantime, the driver would place the reverser in back gear and on hearing the fireman shout "ease up" he would open the regulator and ease the loco into the train. As the coupling slackened the fireman would lift it off the hook, hang up

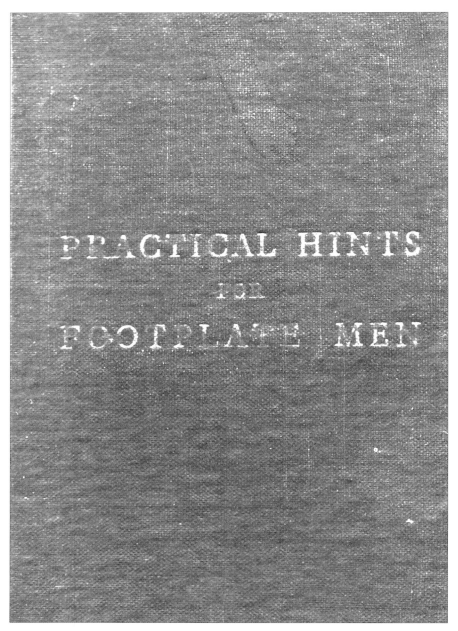

The barely legible front cover of *Practical Hints for Footplate Men* handed to Derek Phillips when a young engine cleaner at Yeovil Town – see page 27 for instance. Designed to be carried in your jacket as an 'instant reference' it explained technical matters as well as 'rules and regs' using photographs and diagrams as well as detailed text.

the steam heat pipes and replace the coach vacuum pipe onto its dummy, job done in one to one and a half minutes. One can imagine a modern-day Health and Safety guru jumping up and down on the spot at the very thought of this practice, but it was done hundreds of times a day throughout the country, and I never heard of anyone getting hurt.

Some fifteen to twenty minutes after arrival, and with all mail and luggage removed from the train and another loco coupled to the country end, the right away tip was given for the empty train to depart for Clapham Yard. Jack pushed hard with '66' to give the train engine, probably an 82000 tank at that time, a good start

out of the station before stopping at the platform starting signal. Shortly the signal cleared and displayed MT (Main Through line) for us to leave Waterloo and run tender first through Vauxhall to Nine Elms Loco Junction Box. Here we ran forward down the incline onto the shed disposal pit. During the waiting time at Waterloo and the short run to Nine Elms I prepared the fire for cleaning.

Now listen up all you 'would be' enginemen! I would try to leave Waterloo with near full boiler pressure and a full glass of water; this would get us to Nine Elms and would see us arrive on the pit with two-thirds of a glass and 160-180lb of steam. The clean (non-clinkered) fire would be

'put up one side'; that is, moved to one side of the firebox (we'll assume the right-hand side) with the long-handled clinker shovel with a few shovelfuls of coal added to the heap to 'burn through' if necessary. During the run to the shed the fire door would be kept shut to conserve heat. We arrived 'on shed' at 12.25am. Once on the pit, the ashpan hopper would be opened and the centre drop section of the grate would be lowered (If this was jammed and would not open, as was often the case, the whole job would have to be done with the clinker shovel via the firebox and cab door). The clinker and ash from the left-hand side of the grate and under the door would be cleared and deposited through the drop section hole into the pit. Once this was done the clean fire would be moved from the right to the left-hand side of the firebox and a few more shovelfuls of coal added to burn through. The right-hand grate area would now be cleared before closing the centre drop section. Finally, the heap of clean fire would be spread across the rear of the grate and more coal placed on top to burn through in preparation for making up the fire before departure.

While on the pit, Jack checked around the engine, topped up the various oiling points, and we took coal and water. After a visit to the turntable there was just time for a cup of tea and a sandwich in the depot mess room. Around 02:00 Jack and I rejoined the engine for a 02:15 departure to Waterloo. After receiving permission, we moved the loco up the short steep climb from the exit road to the head shunt alongside the down local line to wait for the signalman in Loco Junction Box to give us the road back to Waterloo. While we waited for the 02:15 fast Papers to pass on the down main I filled up the back corners of the firebox and dropped a few shovelfuls under the door. The steam coals that we had in those days took a good while longer to get going than the coal we get today and, usefully, we'd stand on the train for around forty minutes at Waterloo. All those bundles of newspapers meant that the gross weight of the train would considerably exceed the tare. I had plenty of room in the boiler for water, so I was taking no chances. The signalman gave us the road and ten minutes later we were coupled to our train and enjoying yet another cup of tea. Our guard arrived and told Jack we had 12 on for 400 tons. Guards became very adept at working out their loads and I imagine that nearly every twelve coach 03:15 Papers to leave Waterloo was assessed as a standard "12 for 400, mate".

Our train consisted of three passenger coaches and nine bogie vans. At that time of year steam heating was 'as required' so some steam was put through the train at the guard's request "just to take the chill off!" The train had been in the station since around 01:30 hours and loading was well underway with large barrows of newspapers being transferred from lorries to the train. Sorters would travel in some of the vans on the train to prepare deliveries for quick dispatch at the later calling points on its journey. During the next thirty minutes or so I gradually made up a large fire until at starting time around three quarters of a ton of coal and fire would be ready to provide the steam to shift an all-up weight of around 600 tons of loco, train and newspapers.

Across the river the hands on the face of Big Ben moved relentlessly towards departure time. There was, for me, always an air of excitement surrounding a departure from Waterloo in the steam era. 03:10 and the final preparations for departure were taking place. Doors were slammed shut, the guard was looking at his watch and the platform starting signal showed a green all clear at the end on the platform. My fire was now burning through well and the injector was on to keep the safety valves from lifting in those last few moments before we started away. And there, spot on 03:15, the guard's green light, "Right away, mate." With the short bout of slipping so characteristic of Bullied Pacifics, Jack and SPITFIRE moved the heavy train away from the platform.

I turned the injector off, half closed the firehole door and sat on my seat, leaning out of the cab window into the cool night air to check the signals on the long right-hand curve leaving Waterloo. With greens all the way through Vauxhall and down past Nine Elms the speed gradually rose until, passing Queens Road, Jack shut off steam for the 40mph restriction through Clapham Junction. As we lurched round the curve through the platform Jack opened the regulator wide and shortened the cut off and I began to regularly feed four or five shovelfuls of coal on and over the large heap of fire under the fire door. SPITFIRE started to do just that – none of the Bullied Pacifics were fitted with spark

arresters and when worked hard they would throw lumps of burning coal small enough to go through the tubes high into the air. It was quite a sight to see! I seem to recall being told that when an attempt was made to fit them with spark arresters it was quickly abandoned after Nine Elms crews threatened to refuse to take them into service, such was the effect on their performance.

We arrived at Woking well up to time and as we stood waiting for station duties to be completed a member of platform staff told Jack that there would be a considerable delay as the diesel that was booked to assist us via Alton had failed and they were waiting for a driver trained on the Cromptons, (D6500s, later type 33s) to sign on at Guildford to bring a replacement to Woking. Now, Jack didn't like doing overtime and

because I signed on early, I was going to have been on duty for twelve hours by the time we got back on shed, so Jack left the footplate and went to 'sort things out'. He later told me that he phoned Control and "told 'em straight, we ain't hanging about here all night waiting for no bloody diesel, we'll go without it!"

The financial penalties for delay to mail and newspaper trains were quite considerable so Control readily agreed that the driver of the failed diesel would conduct Jack as far as Alton, from where Jack knew the road, and ride with us to Winchester to avoid us having to stop at Alton. And so, we departed Woking, near right time, with another 'firework display' up through Brookwood before slowing to take the Aldershot and Alton road at Pirbright Junction. Now, forty-six years later, thirty-six

PRACTICAL HINTS
FOR
FOOTPLATE MEN

•••••••••••••••••••••••••••••

SOUTHERN RAILWAY, TRAFFIC DEPARTMENT (MOTIVE POWER)

Printed for the Southern Railway, Traffic Department (Motive Power) in the late 1940s, 'Practical Hints', in this instance written by Stephen C. Townroe, was in fact a popular theme, growing out of wartime 'advice to the populace' which poured from various Ministries. Booklets could be found covering anything from saving food to avoiding disease.

This is one of the photographs from 'Practical Hints'; it's lost some of its sparkle in the process (it was pretty much lacking in the first place) but is interesting for it was taken at Yeovil Town shed and shows Arthur Hardwick cleaning U class 2-6-0 1790. The 'star' has been burnished into the smoke box door. When I began work as an engine cleaner (the tale begins opposite) 1790 had been renumbered 31790 and was one of the first engines that I cleaned. Arthur was then a driver. I had my first firing duty as a passed cleaner to Salisbury working a U class 2-6-0 on a stopping passenger with him.

show as we stormed up the hill. No problems for steam with a Bulleid boiler, the harder you hit 'em the harder they'd steam, provided the stoker could keep up. Over the next five minutes or so most of my fire was gone, much of it spread over half of Hampshire, but once over the top at Medstead it was all downhill, pretty much all the way to Winchester – our next stop. No problems keeping the engine quiet now, the injector was on most of the way to Alresford. We sailed through the darkened halt at Ropley (nothing much will ever happen there, will it?) at 75mph plus, before slowing to exchange tokens at Alresford. Another little dash (the Mid Hants saw regular high speed running in BR days) through Itchen Abbas before giving up the Tyer's single line tablet at Winchester Junction and dropping down into Winchester City station. We were well up to time and the opportunity was taken to have a wash in the bucket in anticipation of a quick getaway home after getting relief at Eastleigh Shed.

It was now gone five o'clock and Jack and I were both tired – it had been a long night. The guard gave us the tip and we set off on the last short hop to Eastleigh. As we passed Shawford at around 65mph Jack shut off steam and I put an injector on, only it didn't pick up; try again, and still no go, so I attempted to start the other one with the same result. A quick look at the tender gauge confirmed that we had run out of water. Waterloo to Eastleigh with an assisting diesel from Woking would not have required us to take water en route but with the additional trials and tribulations of the journey we had both failed to take into account the extra water usage. 34066 only had one of the smaller capacity tenders and what with the additional blowing off (10 gallons a minute goes out of a safety valve at full bore) and the extra work performed, she had used considerably more water. Had I missed the token at Alton the additional stop and ensuing struggle up the bank to Medstead could have seen us run out of water even earlier.

We now had just over half a glass of water and the safety valve had lifted plus there was no water column on the platform at Eastleigh. As we stopped at the platform, the shunter, walking towards us to uncouple, was probably quite surprised to see me dart in between to unhook. The dummy was off, and we quickly scuttled off to shed. A quick word

of which I regularly drove trains over this route, I know it like 'the back of my hand' but my trip with 34066 was my first one at night between Pirbright and Alton. The Guildford driver was now in the driving seat and punched the engine away from the junction up the climb to Foxhills Tunnel with great gusto. Another firework display! With my limited knowledge of the route there was some 'blowing off' as the engine was eased through Aldershot, and again while negotiating the sharp curve at Farnham Junction. Away we went again with a clear road through Farnham and some fairly speedy running through Bentley. The

Guildford man spoke to Jack, and I was told to 'get some in there' for the climb out of Alton. Jack took over the driving approaching Alton whereupon the Guildford driver said to me "You going to have the token then mate?" And so, it was left to me to stand behind Jack and catch the single line token, at around 35mph. It didn't hurt as much as I thought it was going to, but had I missed it and we'd had to stop to fetch it subsequent events could have turned out quite differently. The reason for the high-speed pick-up was, of course, that we were now faced with the climb from Alton to Medstead. It must have been quite a with John at the blowdown pit, "No chance of a blowdown today mate," and we dropped on to a fortunately unoccupied disposal pit and quickly put the pipe in. I expect the crew on ashpans were also somewhat puzzled by our enthusiasm in taking water for them as well.

So that was it; I had made four hours overtime, again, and learnt another valuable lesson and we had saved the day, just, plus I could now truthfully say that I had been over 'the Alps' in a Spitfire!

Gerald Smallacombe, Okehampton
I began work as an engine cleaner at Okehampton shed or 'Okey' as it was known, on 11 February 1952, at sixteen years old, eventually becoming a fireman and passed fireman until I left the railway service in 1965. We worked trains to Plymouth Friary, Padstow, Bude, Exeter Central, Tavistock South and Lifton. We also had the Atlantic Coast Express from Otterham where we relieved Wadebridge men and worked the train as far as Okehampton where we were relieved by Exmouth Junction men. The engine was always a West Country.

I recall a rough trip during a spell of bad winter weather – late in the 1950s if memory serves. Driver Percy Woolridge and I had worked a train to Plymouth Friary with a T9 4-4-0. When we took the engine to Friary shed, we were told for some reason, that we had to work the Plymouth to Brighton passenger train as far as Okehampton with West Country 34011 TAVISTOCK. My mate and I climbed aboard the engine, where there was an ex-Neasden man called Monk on the footplate. Coal was scarce as deliveries were held up by the weather and the tender had been filled with coal from the depot reserve stock which had been stacked, gently decaying, for years. Coal slowly deteriorates and loses its calorific value if left out in the open in all kinds of weather for many years. Monk told us in no uncertain manner "You won't get there I tell you now." The firebox had been filled up with old rubbish from the tender which was mainly formed of small lumps and coal dust, the fire was glowing a dull red and not burning through as it should have been, with half a boiler full of water showing in the gauge glasses. Nonetheless we had a train to work; the Plymouth to Brighton service was an important train, so we had no choice but to do the best we could in the circumstances. So it was

with some trepidation that we reversed into Friary station and coupled on to our train. The steam blower was on as I stirred up the fire with the dart to try and get some air into the fire and try to 'blaze it up'.

By the time that we had reached our first stop, Devonport station which isn't that far from Friary, we had about 160lb of steam with the water in the gauge glasses bobbing just above the bottom nut. We had to have a 'blow up' before proceeding further, it was 'poke and blow' all the way, with my mate nursing the engine as best he could. It turned into one of the roughest trips that I ever had on a West Country which were normally good steaming engines; the coal was near to useless and how we got over Meldon I do not know. We were relieved (an understatement) to see the distant signal for Okehampton loom into view and we rolled into the station where the relief crew from Exmouth Junction, unsuspecting driver Geoff Josling and fireman Ray Scene, were waiting by the water column to take the train on to Exeter Central.

They knew only too well, from the lateness of our arrival and the hiss from the steam blower as we came to a stop at the end of the platform, that something was wrong. As they climbed aboard we told them the full sad story, though the state of the fire and the bad coal needed little further comment. To put it mildly they were a bit miffed. A telephone call to Exmouth Junction MPD saw to it that a replacement engine would be waiting at Exeter Central for the onward journey to Salisbury. Poor old TAVISTOCK had rallied round somewhat during the brief stop at Okehampton, unexpectedly, as the tender was filled; the Exmouth Junction crew viewed their onward progress with less than relish but, with no alternative, duly set off for Exeter. Meanwhile, my mate and I made our way to our loco shed where a sit down in the drivers cabin and a mug of tea was the order of the day.

We heard later that, when the Exmouth Junction men eventually reached Exeter Central, the formidable figure of Inspector Sam Smith was waiting at the end of the platform and he immediately asked Driver Geoff Josling why he had asked for a replacement engine when theirs was fresh off shed at Plymouth. The driver invited the Inspector to have a look at the contents of the tender which he did, muttered something which suitably expressed outrage. No

more engines were coaled with the old stock at Plymouth Friary and it was discreetly disposed of.

There was much crew changing on the lines west of Exeter. Exmouth Junction men used to work the down Padstow ACE with a light Pacific from Exeter Central and would return from Padstow with a passenger train to Okehampton where they were relieved by Okehampton men. The Exmouth Junction men would moan and groan as they had to work this train all the way from Padstow with an ancient, tottering T9 instead of a West Country which was a more comfortable engine to work on and a type they were much more accustomed to. After being relieved at Okehampton station, the Exmouth Junction men would wait and relieve another Okehampton crew on an up Plymouth, working this train to Exeter Central. 'Okey' crews too, worked passenger trains to Padstow, a distance of 63 miles. Engines as well as crews swapped over at Okehampton and when getting a West Country ready I'd pack the firebox with coal, especially the back corners and under the firedoor; not for nothing were they termed 'coal gobblers' down our way but though in some circumstances this could be true enough, on the journey to Padstow I hardly touched the firing shovel as it was mainly downhill all the way. Coming back was another matter…

Derek Phillips, Yeovil Town
I soon found out during my early days as an engine cleaner at Yeovil Town engine shed that the Bulleid Pacifics were not referred to as such by the drivers and firemen. The bigger rebuilt Merchant Navys after the first one CHANNEL PACKET were the 'Packets' and the air-smooth West Country and Battle of Britain engines were always simply the 'West Countrys.' Although none of the engines was actually allocated to Yeovil Town, at least a couple if not more, could be found on shed daily, arriving off the Salisbury-Exeter main line for servicing – 'squaring up', coaling and so on. It was the case, too, that many of the Yeovil Town duties involved working on the engines in diagrams involving other sheds – this was true of other classes as well. Yeovil Junction a mile or so away on the main line was a principal change-over point for crews and locomotives, with the turntable in constant use. There would be plenty of opportunities for a young

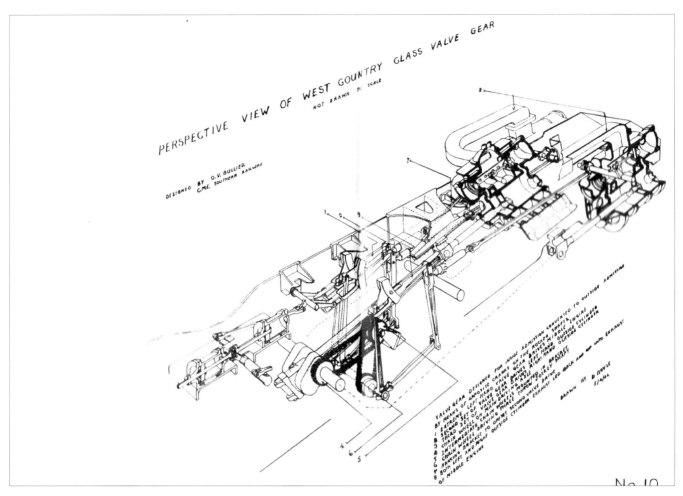

PERSPECTIVE VIEW OF WEST COUNTRY GLASS VALVE GEAR

NOT DRAWN TO SCALE

DESIGNED BY O.V. BULLEID.
C.M.E. SOUTHERN RAILWAY

DRAWN BY D DOYLE
S/KAL

No 10.

'Practical Hints' included a fold-out perspective view of Bulleid chain-driven; this represented a radically different approach to staff education. The reproduction doesn't quite pass muster these days but was a revelation at the time.

engine cleaner to assist a fireman squaring up any type of locomotive standing on one of the disposal pits at Yeovil Town shed. Unsurprisingly, all firemen would be only too pleased to have a cleaner who was willing to learn, clearing the clinker from the firebox raking the ashpan, shovelling char from the smokebox and so on. For as long as anyone could remember cleaners at Yeovil Town were known as 'nippers' and often when walking past a locomotive being squared up on the pit, I have heard the cry 'give us an 'and, nip'. You'd climb up to the very hot cab of a West Country to be overseen by a sweating fireman. An enormously long-handled clinker shovel was used to place the best of the fire to one side of the box thus exposing the clinker on the firebars, which was scooped into the open centre drop grate to drop into the inspection pit. The fire would then be scooped back onto the 'clean' side of the firebox and the process repeated until all of the clinker was removed. The drop grate was closed by inserting the long metal bar into its socket on the cab floor and rocking and clipping the catch

which ensured that the drop grate was locked closed. It was now time to put a few rounds of coal in, under the guidance of the fireman. A low fire would be maintained, just enough to keep the engine in steam, until it was prepared ready for its next duty.

Early on there was the opportunity to master operation of the injectors to place water in the boiler and, armed with the firing shovel and a hand-brush the rather less amenable task of clearing the char from the smokebox. This was an unbelievably dismal job as the fine particles of ash would get absolutely everywhere. All that was available that might be construed as 'protective clothing' might be a pair of bicycle clips to prevent the stuff getting up your trouser legs. The smokebox clear and empty, the door would be closed and the residue swept off the front of the engine. As well as being part of the education and training required of an aspiring fireman, this was also a good chance to meet the firemen at the depot, many of whom excelled at passing their knowledge on to young cleaners. I remember many good

blokes at the depot whom I assisted by helping to square up or prepare locomotives.

During my first summer as a cleaner I was sent 'on loan' with fellow 'nipper' Frank Cannon to Salisbury MPD for two weeks, travelling by train each day. When we arrived at Salisbury station we reported to the chargehand in the drivers' cabin at the London end of the island platform, a small room equipped with a gas cooker with ring, a table and chairs. Inside there were drivers and firemen awaiting the arrival of passenger trains from Exeter to work them forward to Waterloo. The engines worked through, and our job principally was to shovel coal forward on the tenders of the arriving locomotive and to assist with filling the tender with water during the crew changeover, all in the mere six minutes allowed before the train departed.

The cabin air was thick with tobacco smoke; there were extra firing shovels leaning against the wall outside, so as soon we heard the 'clonk' from the connecting rods of a 'Packet' or a 'West Country' resounding along the platform and growing louder as it neared the water column, we picked a shovel apiece and set off. As the locomotive came to a stand with noise and steam from the safety valves resounding into the air we scrambled up on to the tender. One of us would place the 'bag' in the filler hole into the tender while the column was turned on by one of the firemen. It was 'all systems go' as we frantically shovelled as much coal as possible forward in the six minutes before the train departed. 'Shovelling' is actually something of a misnomer, for very often the lumps were far too outsize for a shovel; more accurately the coal was 'manoeuvred' and levered forward. The water bag was thrown out from the tender when it was full (to overflowing) and the tender lid closed. The water column arm was pulled clear by its chain; time for us to climb down and relax, as with a blast on the deep throated whistle which this class of locomotive is equipped with, the 'Packet' set off on its journey to Waterloo with its long, crowded train rumbling along in its wake. Time for us to retire to the cabin where I could enjoy one of mum's glorious 'doorstep' sandwiches. If a Monday then it would be Sunday's leftover roast beef with a dollop of cold onion sauce, very tasty, and a Lyons apple pie my favourite, plus a can of strong tea without sugar. With luck this could be comfortably consumed before the next train arrived, whereupon a repeat of the frantic shovelling ensued.

In the afternoon it was time to walk to the MPD, a few hundred yards to the west. Salisbury was one of the largest sheds on the Southern Region and though it was fairly close, walking was not encouraged to and from the station, unsurprisingly due to the number of trains and light engines, and the shunting in the West Yard. Under the care of the chargehand who also was returning to the shed we were given a lift in the cab of an engine. Upon presenting ourselves at the office we were given orders to report to the shed turners. These were a driver and passed fireman whose job it was, once an engine was squared up, coaled, watered and turned, to stable it in the correct order for its next duty. It was an important job in a busy depot like Salisbury, and all loco sheds had shed turning links. As indicated, the trick was to make sure the engines could get out again in the correct order. We were directed to the disposal pit by

the coaling stage where a whole line of engines were awaiting attention; Bulleids, S15s, an Arthur or two, BR Standards and perhaps a Western Region Hall among others, various tank engines especially. The pit was full from end to end. We were allotted an engine each and told to get on with it and be as quick as maybe! Frank and I back at Yeovil had only had a few attempts at 'squaring up' and that was under the instruction of the fireman who we were helping at the

time. Here at Salisbury we were on our own, and looking back it was the best 'in at the deep end' way to learn. My first engine to square up was a Hall 4-6-0 and there was so much clinker in the firebox it was coming loose and dropping to the floor. The first step was to cut the clinker with the 'dart' then dig the clinker shovel into the firebox, scoop out the clinker and throw it over the side. This engine was in such a bad state that the shed turners decided that the best

SINGLE LINE WORKING

In this picture the Handsignalman is at his post, and the Pilotman is joining the engine preparatory to conducting the train through the single line section.

Another (admittedly a bit murky) image reproduced from 'Practical Hints', illustrating emergency working on a double track line. Single line operation has been brought in, under the control of a pilotman and hand signalman, the former riding on the locomotive which may be working 'wrong line' through a section.

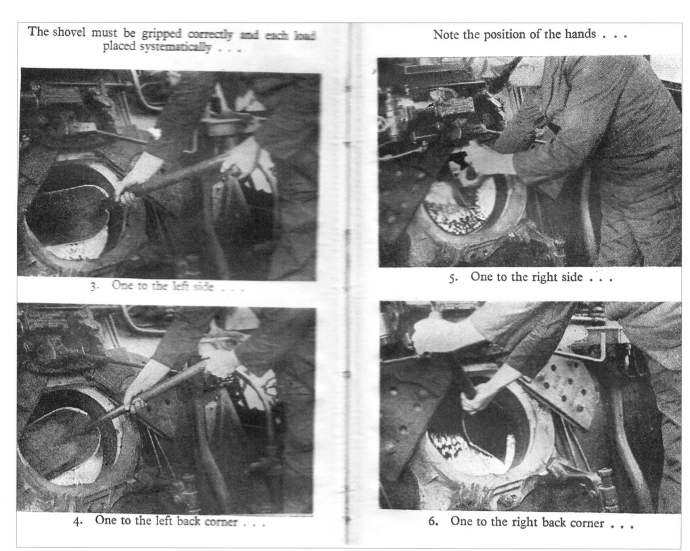

The shovel must be gripped correctly and each load placed systematically . . .

Note the position of the hands . . .

3. One to the left side . . .

5. One to the right side . . .

4. One to the left back corner . . .

6. One to the right back corner . . .

'Practical Hints' on how to fire a Bulleid.

course was to throw everything out and light her up again. By the time I'd emptied the firebox, the turners had thrown some cut up wooden sleepers up on to the cab floor, which were in turn thrown into the firebox with some oily cloths covered in paraffin. There was enough steam in the boiler to give a touch on the blower to bring the fire around with some nice 'rubbly' coal placed on top. There was no time to hang about as I closed the firedoor and, grabbing the firing shovel and hand brush, headed for the smokebox. I climbed up on to the buffer beam, unscrewed the handle and opened the door; the hissing of the blower grew louder and the hot char flowed out. Shovelling out this hot very fine ash was far from pleasant; there was no cover remember so it would blow everywhere or quickly reduce to sludge in heavy rain. Yet by far the most unpleasant job on squaring up was cleaning out the ashpan. I jumped into the inspection pit with its piles of hot clinker and pools of water, trying to avoid burning the

soles of my boots and only succeeded in filling them with filthy water. The ashpan was jammed full and as I raked it out the pit was filled with clouds of choking grey dust.

As soon as I staggered out from the pit, the shed turners moved the Hall to the coal stage where it was duly coaled and watered. The turntable was at the end of the pit line; in fact it was the only way off the pit line whether the engine wanted turning or not, although most did. The more modern engines like the rebuilt Bulleids and the BR Standards were easier, with their rocking grates which cascaded the clinker straight down into the pit. The original West Countrys did at least have one drop grate in the middle of the firebox. On engines older then these, like the Arthurs, S15s and all the rest, everything was thrown out over the side of the cab, an awkward, back-breaking procedure, manoeuvring hot clinker in the confines of an engine cab. Long fireboxes required longer fire irons to reach the end of the box and the

weight of these alone was formidable enough. Tank engines like the Drummond M7s were the worst to square up; there I would be, delicately balancing a piece of clinker on the end of the clinker shovel when bang! the top end of the shovel handle would hit the cab roof and the piece of clinker would drop back into the firebox. Or, swinging the long handled shovel carefully around the cramped cab I would bang my knuckles on the reversing lever or the handbrake handle. But like all jobs I soon learnt the best way of doing things. They were long days at Salisbury but the blokes were a good friendly bunch and always helpful to Frank and me and we both became old hands at squaring up after a couple of weeks. I was to return to Salisbury shed many times as a fireman. Returning to Yeovil Town after the two weeks at Salisbury it was time to resume the normal duties in an engine cleaner's life. Shortly after, Frank Cannon and I were sent to Exeter to attend a two week 'passed cleaner' course under locomotive

inspector Edgar Snow. The first week was spent in a grounded LSWR coach body near the carriage cleaning shed at Exeter Central, learning rules and regulations with other cleaners from Exmouth Junction, Bude and sheds further west. The second week was spent on practical learning regarding steam locomotives at Exmouth Junction. This was followed by a firing test, working a stopping train from Exeter Central to Yeovil Junction under the eagle eye of senior locomotive inspector Sam Smith. On arrival back at Yeovil Town shed I had to answer an inquisition on rules and regulations, plus naming all the moving parts of a locomotive valve gear and their function. After being a 'passed' cleaner for a few months and having a firing turn to Salisbury with a U class 2-6-0 on a stopping passenger train to Salisbury with Driver Arthur Hardwick, my promotion to fireman came through and I was paired with Driver Garth Ostler; his brother Jack Ostler was also a driver at Yeovil Town. Garth and I got on very well, he taught me a lot about firing locomotives and was a good steady driver. I worked at various times with most of the drivers and passed firemen at Yeovil Town including: Den 'Ginger' Rigden, Norman Gosling, Trevor Hayward, 'Captain' Sid Woods, Walt Bird, Jack Hobbs, John Gilham, Harold 'Hammer' Ham, Den Pike, Doug 'Stumpy' Rigden, Fred Martin, Arthur Hardwick, Fred Symonds, Reg Dennett, Charlie Pattle, Bill Godley, Don Willcocks, Don Webb, Vic Burt, Bob Parker, Sid Sprauge, Den Norris, Walt Perry, Maurice Gerrard, Bill Shire, Albert Chainey. Stan Edwards, Ken Perry, Reg Woolmington. Bert Laimbeer, Joe Swaffield, Bert Vickery. The shed links as constituted back then at the end of the 1950s consisted of:
No.1 Link, 12 Duties
No.2 Link, 12 Duties
No.3 Link, 4 Duties
No.4 Link, 4 Duties
Branch Link, 3 Duties
Shed Turners, 2 Duties
Yeovil shunter, 2 Duties.

I also recall the booking clerks in the busy shed office: Reg Bartlett and Jack Kerswell feverishly working at piles of paperwork sorting out daily duty rosters for engines and crews in the days before computers, all to the sound of telephones continually jangling. Of all the types I have fired none could match the Bulleid Pacifics with that oh-so free steaming boiler.

No locomotive has ever been built to suit 100% of the needs of the men who had to work it; however, the Bulleids came very close to achieving that. They were the first in the UK to have electric lighting in the cab and underneath, plus the marker lights on the front of the locomotive and the rear of the tender, with ultra violet lighting in the cab illuminating the gauges and water gauges, all powered by a Stones steam worked generator.

On other classes of locomotives at night, drivers and firemen carried a small torch to shine down from the cab to see if the water pick up on the steam injector was working. On the Bulleids this was not necessary as there was electric lighting underneath the cab to illuminate the injector overflow pipe at night. There were also lights on the driver's side illuminating the reverser and cut-off indicator. The padded seats were welcome when compared to the basic plank on earlier classes. Lest I seem carried away, all was not perfect in the Bulleid garden. There was the chain drive in its oil bath slipping, steam and smoke beating down obscuring a driver's vision, plus the oil-soaked lagging under the air-smooth sheeting at times catching fire. All this has been well documented – laboured even – elsewhere. The late Eric Youldon enjoyed making the point that overheating of the inside big end of the oil bath engines was very rare yet on the rebuilds heat detectors ('stink bombs') were necessary. Whatever the arguments, I loved working on them; they were the finest.

The cab was the best that I have ever worked in, mostly draught free and exceptionally warm in the winter, although it could be a sweat box in the summer. Okehampton's Gerald Smallacombe has already noted (above) that the Bulleids were widely termed 'coal gobblers'. It was the usual practice at Yeovil that when a West Country had been squared up and was going to be prepared almost right away, it would be placed ready for coaling either on the No.1 shed road or the adjacent coal road. The tender access door would be opened, I'd sit on the fireman's seat with feet raised up out of the way; there'd be a warning shout from the coalman and the steam crane would raise a tub full of coal over the tender near to the open access door. The coal duly cascaded through, spilling on to the cab floor. I'd then clear any coal from the door and close and clip it shut, allowing the coalmen to carry on with

coaling the tender. So armed with the coal pick and shovel it would be time to make up the fire, on this type of locomotive the firebox is very deep, so most of the coal on the cab floor would be shovelled into the back corners, a good smack with the coal pick on the larger lumps of coal would do the job of cracking them in half, enabling it to go through the firehole door. So this was not so much a 'top up' as a 'pre-top up'.

When all the coal had been shovelled into the firebox, it was time to clean the cab floor with the 'pep pipe' (a water hose) leaving the fire to burn through. The worst thing as a fireman on this class of locomotive with its air-smooth sheeting was the filling of the sandboxes. There was no running plate and a ladder had to be used to reach each box in turn. I can still remember the one used at Yeovil; part of an old signal ladder, it was usually propped up against the shed wall. If it had disappeared, as happened, you had to search it out. Once found, it would be propped against the side of the engine, while you fetched two 'shutes' of dry sand from the sand furnace inside the shed. Climbing the ladder meant holding on to it with one hand with a shute of sand in the other. It was best to make sure the box door was open before you began as they had a way of sticking shut. In a kind of acrobatic display with a heavy awkward weight, the shute had to be balanced on one shoulder for the contents to be tipped in to the sand box. There were two such boxes each side plus the hand-operated sand boxes on the tender, and they'd invariably be empty due to the well-known slipping propensities of this type of engine. They consumed a lot of sand and quite a few trips to and from the sand furnace were necessary. It was all part of the job of course.

The rebuilt Bulleid Pacifics had a conventional running plate making it easier to refill the sandboxes without resorting to a ladder. Both the injectors on a Bulleid Pacific were on the fireman's side of the cab underneath the seat. Here too were the controls for the pep pipe and the tender spray, both of which only worked when the injectors were working. I soon got used to working the treadle on the steam operated fire door. Placing a round of coal in the firebox on the road was almost balletic, requiring balance and the mastery of repetition. First, position the right foot close to the treadle, swing around to the shovelling plate

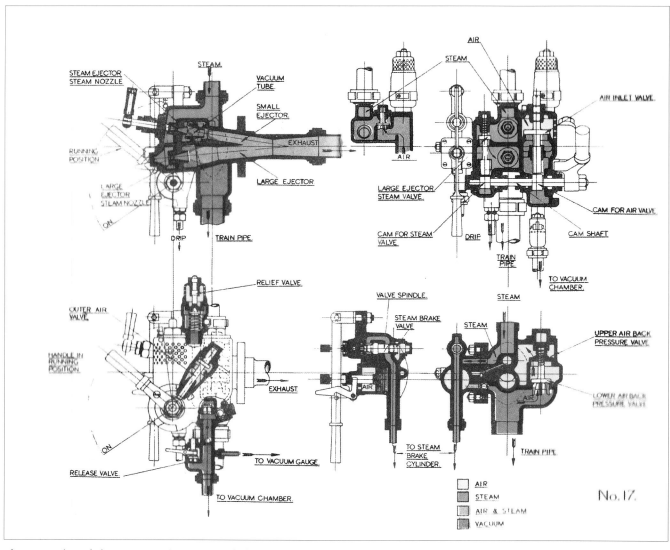

Image labels (clockwise/as positioned):

STEAM EJECTOR STEAM NOZZLE · STEAM · VACUUM TUBE · SMALL EJECTOR · AIR · STEAM · AIR INLET VALVE · RUNNING POSITION · EXHAUST · LARGE EJECTOR · LARGE EJECTOR STEAM NOZZLE · ON · LARGE EJECTOR STEAM VALVE · CAM FOR STEAM VALVE · DRIP · TRAIN PIPE · CAM FOR AIR VALVE · CAM SHAFT · DRIP · TRAIN PIPE · DRIP · TRAIN PIPE · TO VACUUM CHAMBER · OUTER AIR VALVE · RELIEF VALVE · VALVE SPINDLE · STEAM · HANDLE IN RUNNING POSITION · STEAM BRAKE VALVE · STEAM · UPPER AIR BACK PRESSURE VALVE · ON · EXHAUST · AIR · AIR · LOWER AIR BACK PRESSURE VALVE · RELEASE VALVE · TO VACUUM GAUGE · TO STEAM BRAKE CYLINDER · TRAIN PIPE · TO VACUUM CHAMBER

Legend: AIR · STEAM · AIR & STEAM · VACUUM

No. 17.

The mysteries of the vacuum ejector revealed, courtesy 'Practical Hints'.

on the tender, scoop a shovel full of coal, turn around, place right foot on the treadle, opening the firedoor, throw the contents of the shovel into the firebox where needed. Sometimes, inevitably there was a miscalculation and the shovel load of coal met a closed door, much to the amusement of my driver, as the stuff bounced and scattered across the floor. Normally on a stopping train I would open the firedoor manually and would make resort to the treadle on goods trains especially on the steep inclines of the switchback route between Salisbury and Exeter Central. Keeping the back corners filled on a Bulleid was vital, a firing round while working on the 'road' would consist of one shovel of coal to the left side of the box, one to the left back corner, one to the right side, one to the right back corner, one in the centre and one under the door, little and often was the rule.

Yeovil Town was a medium sized shed and we had lots of work, covering many locomotive diagrams. These could be very complex and

would involve two, three or more sets of men from more than one MPD over twenty four hours. Such diagrams or 'Duties' as they were termed had a reference number and those in which Yeovil men were involved in the summer of 1963 are listed herewith.

Yeovil. Preparation and disposal on shed obviously would never involve crews other than Yeovil ones, so this was termed No.1 Duty. The other specific Yeovil Duties were Nos.512, 513, 514, 516, 517, 518, 519, 520 and 521.
Others in which Yeovil men played a part, or in which engines visited the shed were:
Salisbury Nos.461, 471, 478, 479, 480, 497, 500, 501, 503, 505 and 506. Exmouth Junction Nos.544, 545, 546, 547, 548, 550, 551, 561, 584 and 607.

The branch services to Taunton were worked under Yeovil Duty 518 and Taunton Duties 31 and 33: the Taunton-Yeovil goods 6.20am ex-

Taunton came under Plymouth Duty 834 (Taunton men). When the class 22 diesels began working some of the Taunton-Yeovil branch services they were worked by Taunton men under Newton Abbot Duty No.46.

I do not recall ever having a 'rough trip' on a West Country or a serious problem with steaming; however, my driver Garth Ostler and I did have an unforgettable trip one night. We were working on an early morning up goods from Yeovil Junction that we were booked to work as far as Tisbury. It was pouring down with rain. Normally it would have been an S15 4-6-0 on this train, but this time it was a West Country. I was grateful for the enclosed Bulleid cab on a night like this instead of the open cab of a Maunsell S15 4-6-0 which would have had a tarpaulin slung between the engine and the tender. The warm cab was a welcome haven from the wild weather outside. The steam generator for the electric lights was whirring away with the cab lit by ultra violet; these were 'nonglare' and especially designed not to interfere with a driver and fireman's sight during the hours of darkness, just one of the superb features on this class of engine designed by Oliver Vaughan Snell Bulleid.

Garth opened the regulator cautiously and with just a hint of a slip we pulled away with a touch of steam sanding as this was normally a heavy train. Although the engines were equipped with electric marker lights, at night a lit oil head lamp was also carried in the cab to exchange signals with the guard in his brake van indicating that a train was complete. This also served as a tail lamp when travelling light engine. As we pulled away and slowly gathered speed the guard was waving a white lamp confirming that the train was complete and all wagons coupled together, to which I replied with a wave from our headlamp.

The journey through Sherborne and climbing the bank to Milborne Port was uneventful. The signal box was switched out and we ran through the station and downhill to Templecombe where we came to a stand and reversed our train into the

upper yard for the shunting engine to remove wagons and attach others. The yard was packed with wagons and very busy with shunting at the time with trains not only off the main line but from the Somerset and Dorset Joint too.

When all was ready, we set off downhill towards Buckhorn Weston tunnel which at that time was reduced to single line working as contractors were re-lining the tunnel roof. A temporary signal box, named 'Abbey Ford' had been erected at the western end of the tunnel alongside the up main line, and controlled the signals and points at either end of the tunnel. The amber distant signal glimmered out of the darkness as we approached; this was expected as they were fixed permanently at caution. We had hoped to get a clear road through but then the red aspect of the outer home signal materialised. It remained stubbornly at danger, and with a loud curse my mate closed the regulator and applied the vacuum brake. Our engine, and the long train of wagons behind us came to a halt with a lot of banging and shaking and clanking of buffers.

I climbed down from the cab and made my way to the signal box to 'sign the book' in accordance with Rule 55.

This was one of the most important rules, governing the procedure to be observed when crews waited with a train at a signal on a running line. There had been instances when the signalman had forgotten or not been aware of the train's presence, and the consequences had been terrible. The driver would despatch the fireman to the box to remind the signalman of their presence and to confirm that he (the signalman) had placed the safeguards such as collars on the relevant signal levers. The fireman would then sign the Train Register confirming that this had all been conducted properly. Hence the phrase 'signing the book'. It was not invariably necessary to do all this. A white diamond sign on the signal post indicated the presence of a track circuit and our train would show up on the illuminated track plan in the signal box. The signal would have a telephone to communicate with the signalman. Walking to Abbey Ford

Yours truly refilling the tender of one of Salisbury's 'Packets' 35004 CUNARD WHITE STAR at Yeovil Junction on 28 December 1963 with a train for Salisbury while mates from Yeovil Town shed, drivers Harry Churchill, Norman Gosling and fireman Nigel Extance have a natter alongside the water column. 6435 (pannier tanks succeeded the Southern M7 tanks on the 'Auto') on the left has the Yeovil Junction-Yeovil Town push/pull shuttle. C.L. Caddy.

My late brother Nigel Phillips, also a fireman at Yeovil Town, in happier days on the now-preserved 34067 **TANGMERE** at the Town shed in 1964. This was the best job that my brother and I ever had, and it would all be gone within a few years from the time of this photograph.

signal box was quite an experience; the whole area was lit by arc lamps with the din and clamour of pumps and generators working away. There were large wooden huts on the embankment, sleeping quarters for the men as the work was continuous day and night. The signalman informed me that he had accepted a down train which had to clear the single line through the tunnel before we could proceed. I duly 'signed the book' and left the box. As I tramped back, the electric headlights on our engine were shining brightly through the darkness and the lashing rain, the engine was wreathed in steam with the safety valves roaring away, as if to say that she was all ready to go. I climbed back into the warm cab and told Garth the news, and to say he was not too happy about it would be putting it mildly.

I had the firebox crammed full, the incandescent fire filling the cab with heat through the open firedoor. Water in the two gauge glasses was bobbing up and down just below the top nut. The needle in the steam pressure

gauge was quivering on the red line, as these locomotives were not fitted with dampers (fitted in the ashpan, regulating the amount of air admitted) so keeping them quiet was nigh impossible with a full firebox. The cab was thus a warm and cosy oasis of comfort against the wintry elements outside. I was reluctant to put any more water in the boiler as we had an uphill grade of 1 in 100 in front of us. Garth rolled himself a cigarette and lit it while I puffed on a 'Woodbine'. I'd tried rolling my own 'fags' like most railwaymen but preferred them ready-made.

A few minutes later an eerie whistle indicated the arrival of the newspaper train crawling through the tunnel obeying the speed restriction. As the train passed us headed by a rebuilt Bulleid Pacific the driver opened the regulator as he entered the double-track and sped away on his run to Exeter. Now it was our turn. The signal aspect turned from red to green giving us clearance to climb the 1 in 100 through the 742 yard tunnel. I gave a

long blast on the whistle to alert the guard far behind us in his van, my mate opened the large and small brake ejectors. Twin gauges in the vacuum gauge rising to 21 inches released the brakes from the engine and a few of the box vans in the train which were coupled to the vacuum to give us more braking power. The reverser was put into full forward gear and the regulator opened gently with the steam sanding turned on to help with the adhesion. The engine moved slowly forward, the safety valves stopped rising as steam was admitted to the cylinders, then with a mighty roar she slipped, then stopped and started again, then another slip. A huge shower of steam and sparks flew into the dark night air. At the third attempt, she managed to pull away and the regulator was opened wider as we neared the tunnel portal with Garth blowing a long blast on the whistle to warn the men of our approach.

The tunnel inside as we entered was lit by the glare of electric lights. The men stood in groups on the track bed of the removed 'down' track to our right. The noise from our exhaust was amplified within the confines of the tunnel with sparks from the chimney showering down from the roof. We were in full forward gear with the regulator wide open as the engine dragged our heavy train through the tunnel, and then it happened – she slipped, the workmen dived for cover as smoke, sparks and steam flew everywhere. Four times she slipped and regained her feet, by which time we had lost a lot of momentum and were reduced to walking pace.

All this time Garth had the steam sanding turned on to gain traction. If the engine slipped once more we would be in real trouble but slowly we gained the far exit out into the fresh air as we cleared the top of the incline and started to run down the bank towards Gillingham two and a half miles away. The steam sanding was turned off and the regulator and reverser eased back as our wagons pushed us along down the incline. Time to feed the firebox for the severe climb onwards from Gillingham. It had been stirred up with the slipping through the tunnel so I fed the back corners and under the firedoor; the injector was on and trimmed and would be kept on. Steam pressure was on the mark as the green light from Gillingham's distant signal glowed through the darkness and driving rain.

Garth opened the regulator wider as we ran through Gillingham. The severe four mile ascent to Semley begins at the end of the up platform and our speed decreased as we hit into the bank. Using the steam operated firedoor, it was time for the aforementioned routine while working a train on the 'road' – a shovelful to the left side of the box, left back corner and so on. The routine was never forgotten. The steam pressure was holding and the injector feeding water into the boiler enough for our needs as we eased our way up the bank with the rain still lashing unremittingly down. Garth put the reverser forward slightly but not too much as the engine powered its way in fine style, luckily with no sign of a slip. The up distant signal for Semley was always a welcome sight as it marked the summit of the climb from Gillingham. Its green aspect twinkled through the darkness upon our approach, the regulator was eased back as was the reverser as we rumbled through the darkened station and began running downhill towards our booked stop at Tisbury.

Now was the time to tidy up the cab floor, to sweep up any pieces of coal, then wash down the floor using the pep pipe.

With regulator closed we coasted down the bank, Garth braking the engine. The yellow of Tisbury's up distant glowed out from the darkness, then the green from the home signals. We had to pass the end of the platform for our brake van to clear the points of the up yard. Hand lamps waved by the guard and a shunter cleared us to slowly back the train into the up yard, until we were clear of the main line points, coming to a stand with a loud hiss from the vacuum ejectors as Garth applied the brake. I screwed the hand brake on. The Tisbury station master whose house adjoined the goods yard, used to complain if the safety valves on the engine of this train lifted while standing here. With a West Country this was always a challenge and though I made an effort to keep the engine quiet, it was nigh impossible with a box full of fire and a good head of steam. That said, to be fair most drivers, including Garth did not give a fig about the station master, their

view being, that as we were awake at that hour, why not him?

In the event this was the end of the job; it was time to gather up our bags and walk to the down platform to change over with Salisbury men who would arrive with the 5am Salisbury to Yeovil Town at 5.25am (Salisbury Duty No.503). This was a mixed passenger and vans train also worked by a West Country which we'd take as far as Sherborne; there (indicating just how interconnected some Duties were) we'd change over with Yeovil men who had been working the Templecombe Upper shunter at night (Yeovil Town Duty No.514) walk over to the up yard and climb aboard a 'U' class 2-6-0 and shunt the yard until 10.10am when we would leave light engine for Yeovil Town leaving the engine on the pit for the P&D (preparation & disposal) men to square up. Then it would be home to mum and a late breakfast.

All firemen worked with many different drivers; most were good but there were a few you wanted only to see the back of but there was no choice. Yet in my view there were

Nigel Phillips and Driver Tom Mills on the 'Auto' at Yeovil Town. Such was the variety of work at the shed, a young fireman would be on a duty such as this, the Yeovil Town-Yeovil Junction shuttle for a couple of days; the next time he booked on, would find himself on a Bulleid Pacific on the main line.

Yeovil men complained to the LDC (Locomotive Departmental Committee) in 1958 regarding the clinkered condition of a fire on a locomotive which Yeovil men worked onwards from Salisbury. This is the eventual reply from Mr Lelew, shedmaster at Yeovil Town.

engine drivers and enginemen and it was the latter that held my respect as they could balance the reverser and the regulator with great skill without resorting to opening the regulator as wide as possible. Garth Ostler, my first regular driver when I became a fireman, was an engineman through and through, and I enjoyed working with him. He taught me a lot about firing for which I was always grateful. He was sociable too, which helped enormously – some drivers would hardly talk to their firemen, apart from grunting or shouting across the cab as to the position of signals and so on. As I became more experienced I just put up with the very few that worked like that.

The footplate during the hours of darkness was a very different place, not least through the glare from the firebox affecting a man's vision with regard to spotting the dull glimmer of an oil lit semaphore signal. I would open the firedoor with eyes half closed to combat the glare, while other men would have one eye closed. There were all sorts of local difficulties sighting signals in the darkness. Working a goods from Exmouth Junction sidings to Yeovil Junction, for instance involved running down the bank towards Seaton Junction and the best position for spotting the up distant was the fireman's side on a left-hand drive

engine. I can't remember nowadays how many overbridges crossed the line, but it worked like this; unable to see the bridges in the dark, I would count them by sound as we passed underneath. So many stone built bridges would follow one after the other, then a solitary metal bridge. Locomotives made a different sound under metal and stone bridges and as soon as we had passed under this bridge I would peer out from my side to spy the distant signal which would be more than a mile or so away. As soon as I confirmed the green aspect I'd shout across to my mate 'board ok'. He had been braking our heavy train just in case the distant signal was at caution, so would then let our train run as we would be signalled through the up through road at Seaton Junction. It could not have been more different from today's cab comforts and computer control!

One thing that is rarely written about in railway publications (photographs are even rarer) are the crew cabins at engine sheds. At Yeovil they would resound like a parliamentary debating chamber at times. Mickey-taking and gossip of all kinds would be to the fore, all magnified in the larger sheds with more crews involved.

Salisbury shed like Exmouth Junction was a vast place full of noise and bustle with locomotives arriving

and departing. After working an up train from Yeovil Junction my driver and I would leave our engine on the pit to be squared up, coaled, watered, and turned, and walk through the shed to the office. Outside on the wall was a large blackboard and written in white chalk were all the engine numbers for that day alongside their destinations; after checking for our engine number for the return to Yeovil Junction we would amble towards the cabin. Depending on the time of day, the place would be crowded, with crews from many Southern sheds. I am sure that if the painter Hogarth had ever been there, he would have been inspired to draw one of his satirical cartoons – men of all ages shapes and sizes, sitting around the tables some scowling, some happy, many with faces and hands grimy from coal dust, all wearing the standard BR issue bib and brace overalls, and jackets and greaseproof caps. Some of these would be strewn on the table tops which were dirty and covered with tea cans, old tea cups with the dregs, newspapers, stubbed out cigarettes, sandwich crusts and empty crisp bags. The room would be full of noise and chatter and the air thick with cigarette and pipe smoke. More or less friendly arguments would be going on about anything and there would be the

Told that the engine was being withdrawn from service, Yeovil Town fireman Dave Brown dropped the last fire on 35006 PENINSULAR & ORIENTAL S.N. Co at Salisbury shed on 31 July 1964. Fifty-one years later he was reunited with the restored Merchant Navy at Toddington when, on 16 May 2016, President of the Gloucestershire and Warwickshire Railway Pete Waterman OBE formally unveiled the nameplate. Courtesy Dave Brown.

engines and men whom I worked with back in the day. I will never part with it.

Dave Brown, Yeovil Town

My first working experience of a rebuilt Bulleid Pacific came two days after starting work as an engine cleaner at Yeovil Town MPD (72C). Taking a break from cleaning I paused to admire a recently rebuilt West Country standing on No.2 shed road. Driver Arthur Hardwick asked (well, it wasn't exactly a request) if I would oil the inside motion of the engine which he and his fireman Tim Rodber were preparing for duty. Not knowing what he was talking about I began somewhat timorously to decline the request only for Tim to rather forcefully point out that junior cleaners were expected to carry out this job, without demur. It was my second day at work and at fifteen years old, did not come any more junior, so oil the inside motion it would be. Driver Hardwick would tell me exactly what to do from the ground outside.

The engine was already standing over a pit and Tim moved it a few feet to get the inside big end in the correct position for oiling. The handbrake was screwed on, the engine placed into mid-gear and the cylinder cocks opened. A NOT TO BE MOVED board was placed on the front lamp iron. Then it was noticed that the loco was covering the access steps into the pit and the other end was blocked by ashes. It was promptly decided that I would have to slide down feet first between the driving wheels. With considerable trepidation I duly slid through and after regaining my composure (at least partly) I was told to walk along the wet, greasy, unlit pit until I was under the big end – the first I'd seen in my life. To climb up behind it took some thought followed by acrobatic balancing – eventually the big end cork was right in front of me and Driver Hardwick could pass a full oil can through the wheel space. I pulled out the cork and topped up the bearing. Proud of my efforts I was dismayed to hear there was another cork to attend to, further forward on what Driver Hardwick called the strap. I followed the same procedure, then further along there was the connecting rod. At the front was the small end cork; repeat procedure. None of this was necessary on an original oil bath Bulleid I realised a long time later. I eventually clambered out, again through the driving

inevitable game of cards; Solo was the favourite with crews on the Southern Region.

I'd would make the tea from an enormous ever-boiling kettle atop an ancient gas ring. The rule was to keep the kettle boiling at all times so I would top it up after taking my share, then join my driver at one of the long tables. No real comfort, just long wooden forms to sit on, I doubt if the room or the furniture had changed much since Victorian days! It would not be long before my mate and I would be involved in some banter with other crews as we drank our tea and ate our sandwiches followed by a cigarette adding to the already smoke-filled atmosphere, before going out into the shed yard to find our engine and prepare if for our journey home. Happy days that will always linger in the mind.

Approximately sixty-four years ago on the eve of my passed engine cleaner's course at Exeter I was called into the shed office at Yeovil Town

and handed a copy of *Practical Hints for Footplate Men* which I still have to this day, one of the most technical publications in my view ever written on all aspects of working on steam locomotives. Produced by the Traffic Department (Motive Power) of the Southern Railway and written by Mr Stephen C. Townroe in 1947 who himself was the Shed Foreman at Yeovil Town from April 1939 - September 1939 before being promoted to bigger and better positions on the Southern Railway and the Southern Region of British Railways. The book was designed to fit into the pocket of a jacket and measures 6½ inches by 4 inches, has 72 pages plus 12 photographs and 24 pull-out schematic drawings of parts of locomotives, plus much written technical information and rules and regulations etc. The jacket cover is faded now and has seen better days but brings back many memories of my younger days as an engine cleaner and a fireman at Yeovil Town, its

Left. Pete Waterman OBE and Dave Brown, the last British Railways fireman to fire 35006 in revenue earning service, on 31 July 1964 on the unveiling day at Toddington, 16 May 2016. Courtesy Dave Brown.

Below. 35006 PENINSULAR & ORIENTAL S.N. Co. at Toddington on 16 May 2016 impeccably restored by the 35006 Preservation Society. It was a long and arduous task, taking thirty-three years. Courtesy Dave Brown.

wheels; egress, with the added complication of gravity, was much trickier than ingress. During the rest of my time as an engine cleaner, I often got to oil the inside rebuilt Bulleid Pacifics but I never went into or out of a pit through the wheels again in my railway career.

The shed master encouraged engine cleaners to get involved in preparation and disposal – P&D – it was how you learned the layout and functioning of an engine. Early one morning I was co-opted by fireman Mick Colley to help prepare an unrebuilt Bulleid that he and his Driver, Passed Fireman Reg Dennett, were getting ready to work part of Exmouth Junction Duty 549. This was the 7.50am Yeovil Town-Ilfracombe which Yeovil men worked as far as Exeter Central. Over the next few months, Mick taught me how to fire a Bulleid firebox correctly staying on your side of the footplate, which is difficult, if like me you are right-handed but, in the end, I mastered it. Mick taught me everything a fireman needed to know about the Pacifics, for which I was for ever grateful, and we became good friends. So I was pleased when he applied for a driver's job at Brighton and was successful in gaining the job, later rising to train crew supervisor.

After Mick moved away we lost contact until we met at a family gathering when I realised he was my wife's cousin. After this we kept in touch either through family gatherings or over the telephone, our phone calls usually ending with recollections of Bulleid Pacifics. In August 2017 I was saddened to hear that Mick had passed away. On entering the chapel there no hymns or songs; in their stead came the sounds of a three-cylinder Bulleid Pacific pulling away and the sound went on and on. On the coffin (yes you have guessed it) was a picture showing both sides of an unrebuilt Bulleid Pacific with a train. On top was his Drivers hat, a fitting tribute to a long serving railwayman who had a passion for Mr Bulleid's unrebuilt light Pacifics.

As soon as I was sixteen a place became available on the fortnight course at Exeter, the one which Derek Phillips mentions above. There were seven days of 'theory' in a classroom at Exeter Central and three days 'hands on' at Exmouth Junction MPD. The course wasn't residential so all of us came from the South West: three from Barnstaple Junction, two from Exmouth Junction, two from Yeovil Town and one from Wadebridge. On reflection the Wadebridge lad probably lodged at Exeter, going home at the weekend. Our tutor was Inspector Edgar Snow who announced that, from hereon, wherever possible, we were to travel on the footplate on the way home. The Inspector took us to the roster clerk and found what trains were available and who the drivers were. The trains to Yeovil were the 4.30pm (fast) and the 4.35pm (stopper). Les Billings happened to be in the office at the time – "be at Central at 4.20" I was told.

So later in the afternoon I made my way to the platform to find rebuilt light Pacific 34013 OKEHAMPTON awaiting departure with the 4.30 with driver Billings pacing about not looking at all happy. It wasn't the optimum moment for introductions, as the fireman appeared from the depths of the tender. I explained, almost apologetically, how I was supposed to ride with them as far as Yeovil Junction. He was Graham Smith he said, amiably enough. He and driver Billings worked this train regularly as they were crewed together in Exmouth Junction's No.1 Link (the 'main line gang'). The reason for Les' unhappiness was that we had ended up unexpectedly with a smaller engine and tender, due to our Merchant Navy being snapped up ('pinched' in Les' eyes) for an Ocean Liner Express. In those days, liners like the original QUEEN MARY and QUEEN ELIZABETH and other liners were still crossing the Atlantic with a regular service and the passengers had to be got to and from Waterloo. They were heavy trains, often with Pullman coaches and extra luggage. They were not strictly timetabled as it were; arrivals could be delayed by bad weather for instance. Nine Elms put Merchant Navys on these trains as far as possible; the 4.30pm off Exeter was a Nine Elms Duty, No.5, so the engine would have been in Nine Elms in the morning, the ideal time and place to make a swap. Hence our light Pacific.

As I climbed aboard. Les Billings was sat at the controls and I saw the fire was made up with good sized lumps of coal and burning through, the boiler water level was half an inch from the top nut and boiler pressure nearly on the red line at 250psi. Graham told me to sit on his seat and keep my feet up. At exactly 4.30pm on the dot, whistles blow, and we were right away. Once away from the station Les notched up the valve gear and opened the regulator to the roof. The first injector was put on and the 'dart' (a hardly appropriate term for a long heavy lump of iron) was used to help lift the fire. We passed St. James Halt and ran into Black Boy Tunnel; one thing for sure, the fire had been lifted. No.1 injector was still on with the steam pressure hanging on at 230psi but as we passed Exmouth Junction the steam pressure was rising, so the second injector was put on to help maintain the water level, and Graham was checking the fire constantly.

Going past Pinhoe the boiler pressure was 200psi with one injector maintaining the boiler level, the dart was used in the fire again and the pressure increased on the steam gauge. The gradient eased between Pinhoe and Broad Clyst then rose all the way to Honiton except through Sidmouth Junction where it eased, then it was all uphill to Honiton. Driver Billings worked 34013 extremely hard ('thrashed' was the term) and Graham's experience as a main line fireman showed through. It was good to watch how he maintained such a high boiler pressure 220psi, going through Honiton with two injectors on. Driver Billings spoke for the first time since leaving Exeter.
"You'd better put the other injector on mate."
Graham replied "Tell me where it is and I'll put it on."
I took all this in but of course this was a bit of theatre for my benefit. With the valve gear notched right up and the regulator open to keep the water level up we entered Honiton Tunnel. Out the other side, passing the Incline signal box, all of a sudden our situation changed; with the valve gear reset we raced down Honiton bank with the boiler gauge showing three quarters full. A smile returned to Graham's face and, hanging on to his hat, he leaned out of the cab on his side, gestured me over and pointed out the Seaton Junction distant signal. It had a very high signal post and though it could be seen for miles at night, paradoxically it was not so easy to see in the daytime. Catching sight of the signal Graham shouted 'Distant off!' which Driver Billings acknowledges by raising his arm into the air.Belying the doubts expressed at Central, 34013 being in good condition was performing well through Seaton Junction. We were up to maximum line speed, with the water in the correct position in the gauge glass

John Gilham and Gordon Woolmington on Salisbury's 34026 YES TOR at Yeovil Town shed; the jib of the steam coaling crane is above the cab.

next to the engine which afforded welcome extra time to fill the tender. It was full at last, the van doors closed, and with whistles blowing and the green flag waving, they were right away.

Driver Les Billings retired in 1964 and I last met Graham Smith and Edgar Snow at Padding ton station, in 1966. 34013 OKEHAMPTON was withdrawn on 9 July 1967 and cut up at Cashmores, Newport later that year.

In the early 1960s there were high numbers of passengers wanting to travel from Yeovil to Weymouth on Sundays during the summer months, and it was on one of these Sundays that I was crewed with Driver Fred Symonds on unrebuilt 34063 229 SQUADRON. After preparing our locomotive, which was in ex-works condition, we made our way to Yeovil Pen Mill station and after coupling up to eight Western Region coaches, we pulled into the platform to allow the passengers to board the train.

Guard Ron Lodge gave us the 'right away' on a lovely sunny morning, and off we set to Weymouth with one intermediate stop, at Dorchester West. Fred soon had the train up to line speed and as on the approach to Yetminster station the distant signal was 'off,' the regulator was opened to full going through the station. We started to climb Evershot Bank with its gradient of 1 in 52. As we approached Chetnole Halt I paid attention to the fire which had burnt through, and I started filling the back corners, then a few across the front, and a few in front of the fire hole door. Steam pressure had remained on the mark with the injectors maintaining a correct level of water in the boiler.

Rounding the curve at the top and steepest part of the bank we ran on through the tunnel and over the summit at Evershot station. It was now steady progress towards Maiden Newton and Grimstone tunnel for the stop at Dorchester West. This let day trippers make the short walk across to Dorchester South station for connections to Poole and Bournemouth. Things did not go to plan. Fred ran the train really fast into Dorchester West and over-ran the platform by the engine and three coaches. He was adamant that there was nothing wrong with 34063 and directed me back to see the guard who I met coming to us at the front. Ashen faced, he was convinced that the vacuum pipe on the last three coaches were not connected to the rest of the train. On checking, however, I found

with only one injector being used when required. The fire glittering hot, fired on a regular basis, Graham concentrating on the back corners with no need to shut the fire hole door after each shovel full. The gauge was reading 240psi, the situation on the footplate was more relaxed, and I was working one injector as required.

Still up to line speed (and a little bit more) Graham blew the whistle for Axminster and I felt pride and excitement riding at this speed on the footplate of an express engine for the first time. Racing on, we passed Axe and Broom level crossings and were soon in sight of the milk factory at Chard Junction. The gradient then increased, but we were past Hewish Gates before we even felt it. Surging over the summit we dropped into Crewkerne Tunnel and exited it past Crewkerne Gates level crossing. Graham showed me to blow the whistle as we roared past Crewkerne station. It was here that on 23 April

1953 35020 BIBBY LINE, on the same service, infamously suffered a broken centre driving wheel axle. Debris struck the uprights of the platform canopy causing a partial collapse. The ornate cast iron supports were replaced by plain girders, still in place today.

We raced on to Yeovil Junction and Graham suggested I could help take water at Yeovil Junction. We stopped by the water column with practised precision, just 51 minutes after leaving Exeter Central. It had been an outstanding performance by OKEHAMPTON and its crew.

I jumped down off the footplate to the platform and climbed the tender ladder, pulled the water column chain over and put the 'bag' in the filler hole. Looking down I could see the bottom of the tank; now I understood Les' concerns about water capacity! Small boxes from Yeovil firm Aplin & Barrett were taking extra time to load into the van everything to be in order. There was nothing else to do but continue on to Weymouth.

After descending through Bincombe tunnel, Fred made several test brake applications, and we enjoyed a sedate entry into Weymouth station. The incident was reported to the carriage and wagon department who examined the coaches and found badly worn brake blocks with poor adjustment. Adjustments were made, and the coaches returned to Yeovil in the late afternoon on their booked working. Fred Symonds was known as a 'hard hitter' driving locomotives and it dawned on everyone how lucky we had been to stop at Dorchester. If we had not had the braking incident and proceeded gingerly from thereon the entry to Weymouth would have been fraught with danger. Weymouth station is a terminus at the bottom of an incline; we might have gone through the stop blocks and landed up in the station forecourt.

On 31 July 1964 I worked the last part of Salisbury engine duty 461, the 7.30pm Exeter Central to Eastleigh mail train from Yeovil Junction to Salisbury. The engine was 35006 PENINSULAR & ORIENTAL STEAM NAVIGATION COMPANY and the driver Sid Sprague. On arrival at Salisbury we proceeded light engine to the MPD then on to the disposal pit. We were told by the running foreman not to coal or water the engine and just drop the fire as 35006 was now out of service, which came as a big shock to everyone as it was in perfect condition.

I never asked why it was withdrawn and it was only five years since the engine had been rebuilt, so

the boiler ticket could not have expired but it was only two weeks away from the D8XX Warship diesels taking over the workings from Exeter to London. So it fell to me to be the last British Railways fireman to work 35006 in revenue earning service. It was stored at Salisbury for a few weeks where her side rods were taken off, she was then towed to Eastleigh for stripping of all removable parts. 35006 had been a Salisbury engine since it was built in 1941 until withdrawn in 1964 after 23 years in service. 35006 was taken to Woodhams, Barry, South Wales for scrap.

Fast forwarding 51 years, I was on a visit to the Gloucestershire and Warwickshire Railway with a group from Yeovil when we came across dear old 35006 looking brand new, on static display at Winchcombe. Someone spoke to members of the 35006 Society who were in attendance and told them of my association with the locomotive, after a lengthy conversation I was asked if I would attend the renaming when the locomotive entered service the following spring. In April 2016 I duly received an invitation to attend the re-naming of 35006 PENINSULAR & ORIENTAL STEAM NAVIGATION COMPANY. May 16 2016 was the big day and on arriving at Toddington at 10.00am I was introduced to the Chairman of the Society and the President Pete Waterman who came over as a person who had a massive passion for railways. He renamed the locomotive then we were both invited on to the footplate and given a ride from Toddington to Cheltenham racecourse on the first passenger train since restoration. As for 35006, the Society worked against all the odds

and restored a rusting hulk into a working Merchant Navy that will give years of service.

The last steam hauled Atlantic Coast Express ran on Saturday 5 September 1964 leaving Waterloo at 11am with 35022 HOLLAND-AMERICA LINE hauling the down train. The up train had been diesel hauled for the previous two weeks, for crew training. Saturday 5 September was also the actual last day for the ACE. A new timetable was introduced from Monday 7 September 1964, between Waterloo and the West of England which included a two hourly service stopping at intermediate stations in addition to those served by the steam trains. This was the end for Bulleid Pacifics over the routes that we worked from Yeovil. Looking through my 1964 diary, I never worked on any more from the end of July until the following December – even the stopping trains that we used to work with Bulleids were taken over by DMUs.

During my time at the end of the school term a charter train was organised by the boarding schools in Sherborne to transport their pupils that lived in London for their holidays. This train usually ran on two days, and involved Yeovil crews working the trains as far as Salisbury, going up in the morning and another crew working the empty stock from Salisbury to Yeovil Junction. The train formation consisted of ten Bulleid coaches and three large parcel vans. These would be taken to Sherborne late the previous afternoon for loading with luggage, and the total train formation weight would be over 400 tons. On 17 December 1964 I was rostered to work the empty stock of the Sherborne Schools charter from Salisbury to Yeovil Junction with Driver Fred Symonds. Fred, as previously mentioned, had a reputation as a 'hard hitter' and in fact no one at Yeovil Town hit them harder than Fred. If you could keep up with him you gained his respect. I found him good to work with and very amusing at times.

Walking along the platform at Salisbury to relieve men from Salisbury MPD who were running a bit late bringing our train from Waterloo I could hear the clank of the side rods of a Bulleid Pacific and straightaway noticed that the steam blower was full on with the fireman working the fire with a fire iron. There was no smile from the Salisbury driver, who, as we approached

Ron Harding looking out from 35003 ROYAL MAIL at Yeovil Town shed. Ron later transferred to Weymouth. Courtesy Geoff Tucker.

Four enginemen at Yeovil Town shed whom I am proud to have known and worked with during my railway days. Left to right: George Thorn, John Gilham, Harold 'Hammer' Ham and Reg Dennett.

announced that they had had a hell of a rough trip due to Nine Elms filling the tender with the hated coal briquettes, coal dust compressed with a type of cement to an oval a bit bigger than your fist. These were useless unless mixed with 50% Welsh or Yorkshire steam coal. Climbing on to the footplate of 34036 WESTWARD HO I looked straight at the fire which resembled a garden barbecue after the heat had gone out of it leaving a grey dust on top of the fire. After water was taken, much attention was given to the fire, we obtained a full head of steam and the water gauge showed a near full reading. Bidding the Salisbury crew a less than fond farewell, Fred obtained the right away from the guard and our journey westward to Yeovil Junction had begun.

We made it to Wilton South with 160psi of steam with the injector maintaining water with the blower on to stop the cement dust settling on the fire, we were then held at signals waiting for a previous train to clear the section in front of us, after a few minutes we get the road. Off we go heading for Dinton still holding our own with Fred driving very selectively on how much steam he uses. On approaching Tisbury, the steam pressure was at 160psi our water level was ok, then we have a stroke of luck as signals were against us – whatever was ahead had not cleared the section in front. After a brief time attacking the fire, we got the road and with a respectable boiler pressure of 210psi started off for Semley. This we reached quite easily; boiler pressure had dropped a bit, but we had a full glass of water. From

Semley to Yeovil Junction the main line is a bit of a switchback though we started gaining speed down the long straight Semley Bank. Approaching Gillingham (Dorset) 34036 was up to the line speed 85mph. From Gillingham the line rises to about a quarter of a mile before descending to Gillingham tunnel at 70mph with the fire burning brighter due to the draught created up through the firebox due to the increased speed.

Coming out of the tunnel you are in a deep cutting with the gradient still falling until you pass the village of Buckhorn Weston where the gradient rises once again, all the way past Templecombe until about a mile west of Milborne Port station. Steam pressure dropped but we had a full gauge of water under the three-arch bridge going down the Sherborne bank. Then Fred shouts across "Let me know as soon as you get a view of the Sherborne distant signal". With speed increasing, I caught sight of the signal which was 'off'. The AWS bell duly rang and Fred opened the regulator up to the roof (then it dawned on me what he was going to do). With Sherborne station in full view I hung onto the whistle cord right through the platforms with the speedometer reading 95mph. Fred shook his head – he was trying for the Ton! I thought we had done very well to achieve 95mph taking into consideration how we were struggling at the start of the journey. On arriving at Yeovil Junction, we stabled our train in the down sidings and turned the engine on the table ready for the second Sherborne Schools charter the next day, then light engine to Yeovil loco. We both

agreed that due to diesels now being in charge, this would be the very last time that we would ever work on a Bulleid Pacific. 34046 WESTWARD HO was that locomotive. Driver Fred Symonds took redundancy and left the railway service when Yeovil Town Motive Power Department closed in 1967. I transferred to Old Oak Common in 1965.

Arthur Turner, Bath Green Park

I met the late Arthur Turner way back in 1990 at his home in Bath while researching a book on the S&D and he recalled his days with the West Country class. *Derek Phillips.*

I had my first encounter with a West Country when I was firing to Driver Albert Williams. We'd known each other for many years and were nearly the same age. We had relieved an S&D passenger set and we had to do some shunting at Bath station. A West Country was on the job, and Southern Inspector Jack Hookey from Bournemouth was on the footplate to show us around. He did so, and after a couple of moves, my mate declared "We've got the hang of this," so the Inspector left us to it. After shunting we took the engine to shed and disposed it, and we did this every day for a week.

On the following Saturday we were booked 'passenger' to Bournemouth and return to Bath with pigeon empties from Christchurch or Pokesdown. Upon booking on, my mate was told to work the 'Pines' (Pines Express) to Bournemouth as the driver had injured himself and was at the hospital for treatment. Albert and I walked over to the engine which was standing on 'Tommy' sidings. It was a West Country and we climbed aboard to go to the station. The fireman, a Bournemouth Central man, was a stranger to the road and looked rather weather-beaten. My mate said to me quietly "We can manage this" so I asked the fireman if he would like to ride home on the cushions. He readily agreed. So off we went on this engine, having never had one on a train before, and after a little while my mate wanted a go on the shovel, so we changed over. The problem was that neither of us had a timetable, so we did not know where to stop. We called where we thought we ought and no one complained. We arrived on time so it must have been all right. I had many trips on these engines after this, and even had Albert assisting me with one, and myself driving, from Bath to Bournemouth about 3.30am on a summer service.

One Saturday I was booked to drive 4F 0-6-0 44146, heading another engine on the 10.30am Bath-Bournemouth as far as Evercreech Junction, with fireman Fred Spurrell. On approaching Binegar the distant signal was at caution, and we came to a stop at the home. Trouble ahead! Stationmaster Norman Down instructed me to unhook from the train engine behind us and proceed gingerly into the section armed with a 'wrong line' order. The train in front (the 9.55am Bath-Bournemouth local) had failed and we would have to pull it back to Binegar, along with its engine. Getting the order and formal permission from the signalman we set off, found the casualty, coupled up and dragged the train and its disgraced engine back to Binegar. There, we placed the cripple, 34041 WILTON, in the siding, and we were able to run round and put our 4F on the front of the failed train. The crew off WILTON took over the 4F and sailed off with 44146 at the head of the by-now much delayed 9.55. After a while our original train followed on with just a single engine (another West Country, if memory serves).

We were required to stay behind and attend to the errant WILTON. To our alarm, its tender tank was all but dry; luckily the fire was dying down anyway and we shovelled it out as quick as maybe onto the ground below. There was no choice as to where we did this, for the engine could not move under its own power. Panic over, I took a look underneath – plainly some valve gear was adrift. I telephoned Bath Loco Depot to this effect and eventually senior fitter George Adams and his mate turned up, hurrying down by road (Bath was only a few miles distant) and made sure that everything was ready for the engine to be pulled back to Bath and

we all settled down to wait for the necessary engine to come. Before that, however, in a short while Mr Ivo Peters and Mr O.S. Nock and their families arrived, along with the famous Bentley; both of course were keen railway photographers and enthusiasts and a number of photographs were taken. Ivo Peters was firmly plugged in to the S&D 'bush telegraph' and would have been informed of the events unfolding at Binegar almost a quickly as the shed fitters! They remained, chatting, until we were rescued by driver Harold Barber and his fireman Cecil

Beale with Black 5 44839. They had been forced to wait until the surge of traffic had waned and an engine could be found. The 4-6-0 with WILTON in tow went back (both tender-first) to Bath. On the following Monday, I was invited to peer into the oil bath sump of the West Country, at the broken chain drive which had caused all the trouble.

Bob Cartwright outside his home where he lived with Mum and Dad in Victoria Road, Woolston, Southampton, about to cycle the ten or so miles to Eastleigh MPD: 'I left school in April 1962 at 15 and two weeks later started as an Engine Cleaner at Eastleigh shed. We were not officially allowed to do firing until we were 16, but as the senior cleaner after about nine months I was doing shed shunts and so on due to the extreme shortage of staff at the time. When I officially passed, I jumped in seniority over the older lads that started after me and went straight into the 'Tank Gang'. During the last two years of steam, I was in the Holiday Relief Gang covering all the Links at Eastleigh. I got a Driver job at Waterloo in 1976 and retired from full time work in 2012 after 50 years and 2 months.' Courtesy Bob Cartwright.

Ashford on 11 March 1961 with a variety of locomotives, including a Schools 4-4-0 and a Bulleid Pacific carrying a NOT TO BE MOVED board sharing the road on the left. The shed closed to steam in 1962, remaining open for the servicing of diesel locomotives until 1968. Nick Nicholson, transporttreasury

Only a couple of months old, 21C129 is in malachite green and not yet named, at Ashford on 6 July 1946. R.C. Riley, transporttreasury

'BULLEID SHEDS'
And one or two other locations

ASHFORD
Ashford shed was built by the Southern Railway as one of a number of pre-War modernisation programmes. While Pacifics from other depots were frequent visitors, none was allocated until 1961 when three appeared for a brief period in 1961, one year before closure to steam: 34061 (05/61-11/61) 34070 (05/61-11/61) 34083 (05/61-11/61).

Dover's grimy 34083 605 SQUADRON passes Paddock Wood with a down express on Saturday 10 June 1961. The third rail is in place, for the commencement of electric services on the South Eastern main line just a day or so later, on the following Monday. Electrification saw a number of steam engines (those not immediately redundant) make the trek west; for 34083 this meant Exmouth Junction. Ron Smith, transporttreasury

21C155 FIGHTER PILOT in malachite green, prepared inside Ashford Works on 4 October 1947 for the 1847-1947 Centenary Exhibition. J.C. Flemons, transporttreasury

34073 249 SQUADRON with its Dover shed shed plate 74C on the smokebox door, at Victoria station in October 1957. Jim Flint and Jim Harbart, transporttreasury

DOVER

The six road modern shed at Dover opened in 1928 replacing the former LCDR depot at Dover Priory dating from 1861. Some 360ft long by 100ft wide it was built on partly reclaimed land to the west of the Marine station; like Ashford and indeed all the big modern SR sheds, it was built in ferro-concrete with a northlight pattern roof. There was the usual 65ft turntable and (manual) coal stage. It was but part of a major scheme which included the enlargement of Priory station and the removal of the 60 yard Archcliffe Fort tunnel, which in turn required the excavation of 75,000 tons of chalk. Approximately fifty engines were allocated to Dover which was also responsible for the outstation at Folkestone Junction where the R1 0-6-0 tanks (later replaced by WR pannier tanks) used for banking on the Folkestone Harbour branch were kept. Due to enemy shelling from the French coast during the second world war the depot was virtually out of action with its duties transferred to Ashford. There can be few if any large depots like this, once surrounded by so many anti-aircraft guns. Three Merchant Navys; 35028, 35029 and 35030 were allocated by October 1949 though 35028's stay was relatively brief, the engine moving away to Stewarts Lane in March 1950. 35029 and 35030 were transferred to Nine Elms in June 1955. Light Pacifics were allocated from 1948, with a few having a brief stay and some appearing more than once.

35029 in 'exhibition' condition, plates covered, at Eastleigh on 27 February 1951 awaiting its naming ceremony on 1 March when its ELLERMAN LINES plates will be unveiled at Southampton Docks by Mr A.F. Hull the Chairman of the Line. 35028 CLAN LINE, 35029 ELLERMAN LINES and 35030 ELDER-DEMPSTER LINES were allocated to Dover in October 1949 to work the heavy Night Ferry and other Continental expresses. 35028 was moved to Stewarts Lane in March 1950, with 35029/ 35030 reallocated to Nine Elms in June 1955. 35029 nowadays is a sectioned exhibit at the National Railway Museum. York. This was controversial, and years after the BR Officer deputed to select a suitable candidate from the engines at Barry was reluctant to own up to it! A.E. West, courtesy Mike King.

Dover shed on 23 May 1959. Shakespeare Cliff with its tunnel below looms in the distance. Few very good photographs exist of the shed, peculiarly – maybe it was its site, lying east-west so that the light was often 'wrong'. The coal stage was unusual in that it was constructed entirely in ferro-concrete; it also had an unfeasibly long approach ramp. Dover would certainly be in the running for 'shed closest the sea' for the waves lapped just a few yards beyond, to the left; in gales sometimes, work on the stage had to be stopped for the duration. One Bulleid light Pacific is visible among several former SECR engines and a diesel shunter. R.C. Riley, transporttreasury

Previously at Dover and on the books of Stewarts Lane since March 1950, 35028 CLAN LINE in original state is absolutely pristine, a condition further enhanced by the striking Golden Arrow regalia. It is being coaled and oiled before returning with the afternoon service from Dover Marine to London Victoria. The train was worked by Stewarts Lane men as that depot's Duty No.4. RailOnline

Dover's 34103 CALSTOCK and Ramsgate's 34076 41 SQUADRON arriving at Victoria in 1957 on the Night Ferry with its distinctive blue 'Wagon Lits' sleeping cars. Until the inauguration of the Eurostar services in November 1994 this was the only through passenger train between the UK and continental Europe, from London Victoria to Paris Gare du Nord via Dover and Dunkirk. During shunting on to on the ferry the carriages were arranged into sections and loaded equally on tracks port and starboard on the vessel. Beginning in 1936, the train ran for forty four years, apart from the War, resuming on 15 December 1947 until finally withdrawn in October 1980. The luggage vans behind the locomotives had arrived from the continent with the rest of the train. The distinctive headboard had a blue background. From June 1957 a through carriage to and from Brussels was attached at Lille, hence LONDON PARIS BRUSSELS on the board; prior to this it bore just LONDON PARIS of course. By contrast, passengers on the Golden Arrow made the Channel crossing as foot passengers. transporttreasury

Ramsgate's 34027 TAW VALLEY, the second light Pacific to be rebuilt (in September 1957) arrives at Chatham with the 1.15pm Cannon Street to Ramsgate on 21 March 1959. Lens of Sutton, Denis Cullum Collection.

RAMSGATE

Sited west of the station and north of the line, Ramsgate was another modern shed built by the Southern in the new ferro-concrete. This new material fell rather short of expectation and decay and leaks proliferated at all of them in later years. Faulty detail design and subsequent lack of maintenance were the causes. The new depot, authorised at a cost of £55,000 in 1926 was but part of a vast scheme to modernise the railway in this corner of Thanet – new stations, goods depots, realignment and so on. The SER line between Ramsgate and Margate closed completely and the LCDR route via Broadstairs was connected to the line from Minster by a new 1½ mile connecting line; there were two new stations, Ramsgate and Dumpton Park, opened in July 1926. The former terminus at Ramsgate Town closed from the same date.

The six road engine shed came fully into use in 1930 and unusually had a mechanical coaling plant. Water quality was poor in the district and a 10,000-gallon water softener was authorised in 1933.

By the middle of February 1946 there were half a dozen or so Bulleid Pacifics at Ramsgate for the principal London trains: 21C119-21C125. The number had risen to twelve by January 1947.

The Kent Coast Electrification of 1959 brought about the loss of the shed's regular allocation, reducing it to a stabling point, servicing visiting locomotives from Bricklayers Arms, Ashford, and Dover. During the following year, the shed building itself was taken over for conversion to EMU maintenance with the steam locomotives serviced and stabled in the open. The shed closed to steam operation in December 1960.

34086 (later 219 SQUADRON) comes into Ashford past the 'D' signal box, with an up train on 8 July 1950. A.E. West, courtesy Mike King.

41

34080 standing alongside the down platform at Ashford on 8 July 1950. The as-yet not named locomotive is attached to 'chocolate and cream' 'Ironclad' Set 237 which also included restaurant car 7934 plus two loose coaches (eleven vehicles) dating from the 1948 summer services when British Railways, as part of a publicity exercise, painted a certain number of coaching sets in 'plum and spilt milk' or chocolate and cream that were distributed throughout the country for the public to view and voice their opinions. It's hard to imagine such an exercise today, or if there was, whether anyone would bother to look! 34056, 34064 and 34065 were painted in the experimental apple green livery in 1948 to haul the chocolate and cream coaches exclusively on the Chatham line services: 7.20am Ramsgate-Cannon Street, 5.15pm (SX) Cannon Street-Ramsgate, 1.15pm (SO) Cannon Street-Ramsgate, 9.40am (Suns) Ramsgate-Victoria, 3.15pm (Suns) Victoria-Ramsgate. A.E. West, courtesy Mike King.

34081 92 SQUADRON at Waterloo Eastern with the down 'Man of Kent' on 1 August 1957. Lens of Sutton Association, Denis Cullum Collection.

34087, still to be named, in experimental apple green livery at Ashford on 8 July 1950. A.E. West, courtesy Mike King.

34066 SPITFIRE passes Swanley on 9 May 1949 with the 11.30am Ramsgate to Victoria. 34066 was involved in a serious accident, colliding with the rear of a stationary electric train on the evening of 4 December 1957 near St. Johns station, Lewisham in South East London resulting in the deaths of 90 people and injuries to nearly 200. The strangely shaped concrete components are platform supports for some imminent lengthening work. Lens of Sutton Association, Denis Cullum Collection.

Right. An expectant crowd of onlookers gather for the unveiling of s21C170 MANSTON at Ramsgate station by Lord Balfour of Inchrye on 9 March 1948. Naming ceremonies were, where possible, enacted 'locally'; Manston RAF station for instance was located in the Isle of Thanet and thus very much in the 'front line' of the Battle of Britain. Light Pacifics were taken to the nearest relevant station and when there was no obvious geographic connection a ceremony at somewhere like Waterloo would be deemed appropriate – LORD BEAVERBROOK, HURRICANE and SPITFIRE were all named there together for instance in September 1947. MANSTON when named was in malachite green with yellow bands, retaining its Southern Railway number on the cabside with BRITISH RAILWAYS on the tender. Note the Ramsgate coaling plant towering above all. Courtesy Southern Locomotives Ltd.

Grouped on the front of a gleaming MANSTON after the ceremony on 9 March 1948 are, left to right: Mr Horace Moore Shed Master, Mr Fred Porrit boilermaker, Mr Horace Futter Chargehand fitter, all of Ramsgate shed, unknown and Mr Sabine, the Station Master. The 's' prefix disappeared when the locomotive was renumbered 34070 on 31 March 1949. Courtesy Southern Locomotives Ltd.

Flags celebrating the forthcoming Coronation at Westminster Abbey on 2 June 1953 of Her Majesty Queen Elizabeth the Second are draped on the frontage of the Marks & Spencer and Bon Marche stores as 34080 74 SQUADRON approaches Brixton station with the 10am Victoria to Dover on 23 May 1953. Lens of Sutton Association, Denis Cullum Collection.

Ramsgate's 34083 605 SQUADRON approaches Sevenoaks with the 1.15pm Charing Cross to Dover on 23 May 1955. Lens of Sutton Association, Denis Cullum Collection.

34012 LAUNCESTON, previously at Nine Elms, was allocated to the 'Brick' after being rebuilt in January 1958. Peter Fidczuk Collection.

BRICKLAYERS ARMS

The only shed named after a pub, I think it's safe to say, Bricklayers Arms in South London was a curious collection of buildings at the end of a spur line which had grown up in an *ad hoc* way over many years. The Southern carried out a number of improvements including the construction of a large repair shop in 1934 comprising a wheel drop, overhead cranes, wheel lathes etc, enabling work to be carried out on the largest locomotives, which none of the other London sheds were able to do. A number of light Pacifics were allocated to Bricklayers Arms at various dates 1957-1962.

Left. 34013 OKEHAMPTON arrives at Chatham station with the 12.45pm Cannon Street to Ramsgate on 21 March 1959. Lens of Sutton Association, Denis Cullum collection.

Below. Ramsgate's s21C170 MANSTON in malachite green on the Bricklayers Arms turntable on 18 May 1948. During the fifth month of nationalisation the locomotive has BRITISH RAILWAYS on the tender, despite retaining its SR numbering, and the roundel on the smokebox. They disappeared upon renumbering as 34070, once more at Ashford, in March 1949. Another Ramsgate locomotive, 34073 249 SQUADRON can be seen around the corner on the left. The high blank wall, ugly with corrugated asbestos sheeting, belongs to the Repair Shop established here by the Southern in the 1930s. It operated as a sort of 'branch works' for the London area – such facilities, oddly, had been poor at the big London sheds for many years. RailOnline

47

One of Ramsgate's light Pacifics 34076 41 SQUADRON, in BR green on shed at the 'Brick' on 11 October 1952. L.R. Freeman, transporttreasury

34003 PLYMOUTH passes St. Mary Cray on 28 June 1958 with the 1.15pm Cannon Street to Ramsgate. Lens of Sutton Association.

34014 BUDLEIGH SALTERTON leaving Clapham Junction on 23 June 1961 with the 6.10pm Victoria to Brighton via Uckfield. At Exmouth Junction since new, the engine came to Bricklayers Arms in early 1958, upon rebuilding, and stayed till July 1962 – during that time it would seem (see it in the next picture at London Bridge for instance, a year earlier) it seldom if ever saw so much as a hint of a cleaner's cloth. Lens of Sutton Association.

A couple of years before, 34014 BUDLEIGH SALTERTON newly rebuilt would have shimmered in the sunshine but the 'Brick' was a London depot where it was difficult, nigh on impossible to get sufficient cleaning staff. Hence its grimy state (see previous picture too) at London Bridge with the Man of Kent on 23 April 1960. Lens of Sutton Association.

34050 ROYAL OBSERVER CORPS immaculate at Waterloo station on Sunday 2 July 1961 after receiving cab side 'long service awards' in a ceremony for the Royal Observer Corps. The locomotive departed with the 11.30am to Bournemouth conveying members of the ROC. John Eyers, courtesy South Western Circle.

34004 YEOVIL awaiting departure from Cannon Street on 3 May 1959 with the 12.45pm SO to Ramsgate. RailOnline

The shed at Brighton was a joy to behold off the platform end and the lad with his big brother's duffle coat and the let down trousers is taking it all in. This is a Sunday in 1961 so the shed is well-attended with a wide range of locomotives stabled in the yard. That's the tender of 34019 BIDEFORD in the centre foreground, on the hoist and wheel drop road. Jim Flint and Jim Harbart, transporttreasury

BRIGHTON

Brighton shed opened by the LBSCR in 1861 stood close by the station, occupying a cramped site in the fork of the lines to Worthing and Haywards Heath. It was big, with fourteen roads, each of which had an individual arched entrance. Over long years it grew dilapidated and the Southern carried out various improvements to the roof, the yard and so on. The shed had around eighty locomotives but lost importance with the electrification of the main line from London in 1932. Plenty of light Pacifics found their way there at various times between 1948 and 1963. The entire Pacific complement, 34012, 34013, 34014, 34019, 34027, 34057, 34063, 34089 and 34100, was transferred away *en bloc* to Salisbury in September 1963, bringing an end to Bulleids at Brighton.

Below. 34055 FIGHTER PILOT at Brighton on 16 April 1961. As 21C155 it had been named by Group Captain Douglas Bader at Brighton station on 19 September 1947. 21C153 SIR KEITH PARK and 21C167 TANGMERE were also named at the station on the same day. Nick Nicholson, transporttreasury

34008 PADSTOW at London Bridge on 9 April 1962 with the 4.40pm to Brighton. Larry Fullwood, transporttreasury

34047 CALLINGTON arrives at Brockenhurst on a very rain swept 28 March 1958 with the 1.50pm Bournemouth to Brighton. John Eyers, courtesy South Western Circle.

34098 TEMPLECOMBE heading for Bournemouth West from Bournemouth Central, on the final lap of its journey with the 10.00am from Brighton on 21 February 1960. The Brighton engine was booked into Bournemouth Central MPD for engine requirements and used the turntable there, returning tender-first to Bournemouth West carriage sidings to collect the stock and propel it into West station for the return trip to Brighton. The turntable at Branksome had been removed in 1954 but even if it had survived would have been too small for a Pacific. All the S&D engines would turn on the Branksome triangle and also some engines coming down from Waterloo to Bournemouth West and returning from West to Waterloo. The distance between Brighton and Bournemouth is about 60 or so miles, so a West Country with a full tender from Brighton could do the return trip easily without taking on more coal. Waterloo to Exeter services went from start to finish without taking on more coal until they reached Exmouth Junction. We used to have a Sunday night duty relieving an Exmouth Junction crew at Yeovil Junction with an up stopper with a West Country; when we eventually arrived at Salisbury MPD we could not take on more coal as being a Sunday the coal stage did not operate until midnight. After turning etc we returned to Yeovil Junction with a goods and were relieved by another Yeovil crew who worked the train to Exeter with just about enough coal to get there! John Eyers, courtesy South Western Circle.

Brighton's 34055 **FIGHTER PILOT** leaving Salisbury with the 2.53pm Plymouth to Brighton on 16 July 1960; the 1.20pm from Bournemouth West is alongside the bay platform on the left. John Eyers, courtesy South Western Circle.

Stewarts Lane was hemmed in by running lines and viaducts, the latter giving it a labyrinthine look. It was thus a challenge to modernise the place so that engines proceeded conveniently from coaler to turntable and back again without hindrance to other movements. It was accomplished, in the event, with some considerable ingenuity, it should be said. A resident of Stewarts Lane since new to traffic in September 1949, 34092 CITY OF WELLS is standing underneath the mechanical coaling plant on 25 August 1950. It was named WELLS at Priory Road station in Wells Somerset on 25 November 1949 and CITY OF WELLS plates were substituted in March 1950. A.E. West, courtesy Mike King.

STEWARTS LANE

Stewarts Lane MPD had its origins in the early 1860s with the opening by the London Chatham & Dover Railway of a running shed for locomotives and a carriage works at the former Longhedge Farm in south London. The new shed was a semi-roundhouse with *forty* roads half of them covered, radiating from a 45ft turntable, with workshops in a building adjoining the south side. Locomotive works and a goods depot also opened in 1862, the whole complex being known as 'Longhedge.' Further changes came in 1881 with the semi-roundhouse demolished and replaced by a 16-road single ended shed built in brick with a slated pitched roof; this was the shed that existed into BR days. With a hundred or more engines, it became the principal locomotive depot for the South Eastern & Chatham Railway when the South Eastern Railway and the LCDR amalgamated in 1899. As it did almost everywhere across its system, the Southern Railway made a series of important improvements during the 1930s, which included moving some fifty engines from the old LBSCR roundhouses at nearby Battersea Park to Stewarts Lane. This meant that by 1934 one depot, Battersea/Stewarts Lane, provided motive power for both the Central and Eastern sections. To deal with the complement of one hundred and seventy locomotives a thoroughly modern depot was created, laid out to service engines sequentially in the modern fashion of the times. A 65ft turntable was provided on a new more convenient site, the approach roads modified, a 300 ton mechanical coaling plant constructed, a new 20,000 gallon water softening plant installed supplying ten water columns instead of the previous two and the roof was replaced with one of a northlight pattern. The shed was now generally known as Stewarts Lane; it had the largest allocation of any shed on the Southern Railway. The steam locomotives began to dwindle from June 1959 with the opening of Phase 1 of the Kent Coast electrification and Saturday 13 June was the last Saturday of full steam working on the ex-LCDR lines to Dover and Ramsgate. Most boat trains remained steam hauled for the present, however, with Stewarts Lane retaining a dozen or so light Pacifics plus thirty other engines. Phase 2 of the Kent electrification two years later was to see a drastic reduction to approximately 25 engines in 1961/2. The shed, known to railwaymen as 'Battersea' or the 'Lane' had at its peak a staff of 545 including 300 drivers and firemen. It closed to steam September 1963.

Stewarts Lane had the following Bulleid Pacifics on its books amongst its 131 strong locomotive fleet in January 1947: 21C133, 21C134, 21C135, 21C136, 21C137, 21C138, 21C139, 21C140; others came and went over the years too numerous to mention.

35025 BROCKLEBANK LINE in blue livery with the Night Ferry headboard turns at Stewarts Lane MPD on 25 August 1950. 'The Ferry' recommenced running after (obviously) its suspension during the War, on 15 December 1947. It was always a heavy train, with L1 4-4-0s acting as pilots should there be more than three sleeping cars in tow. A.E. West, courtesy Mike King.

Above. 34070 MANSTON with the Thanet Belle headboard standing underneath the 300 ton mechanical coaling plant on 25 August 1950. 34070 is still in Southern Railway malachite green, the last so painted; it stayed in this guise until repainting by BR in March 1953. A.E. West, courtesy Mike King.

Left. 34071 601 SQUADRON on 22 July 1951 in malachite green livery with yellow bands, staying as such until repainted BR green in January 1952. It is standing alongside N class 2-6-0 31810, another Stewarts Lane resident of the time. A.E. West, courtesy of Mike King.

34092 CITY OF WELLS with an up express at Ashford on 8 June 1950. I can recall firing this engine at Yeovil Town many years later after it had been transferred to Salisbury in May 1961. A.E. West, courtesy Mike King.

Diverted due to flooding at Birchington, 34104 BERE ALSTON has the 9.6am Victoria to Ramsgate at Deal Junction on 8 February 1953. 34104 was the last Bulleid Pacific to be rebuilt, in May 1961. Lens of Sutton, Denis Cullum Collection.

34104 BERE ALSTON passing Canterbury 'A' Junction on 28 February 1953 with the 11.21am Birchington to Victoria. Lens of Sutton Association, Denis Cullum Collection.

35028 CLAN LINE in BR green stands at Folkestone Junction on 26 May 1954 after arrival with the down Golden Arrow, the driver and fireman looking a bit nonplussed at the photographer's presence. As always, the engine with 'the arrer' has been immaculately turned out by Stewarts Lane. The *flèche d'or* on the casing was an incredible fifteen feet long and thus suited to the air-smooth locomotives. The rebuilt Bulleid Pacifics and the Britannias carried a smaller version of the arrow, on the smoke deflectors. John Head/Rail Archive Stephenson.

Stewarts Lane-allocated 34100 APPLEDORE in a grimy external condition passing St. Mary Cray Junction with the 1pm Folkestone Harbour to Victoria on 6 June 1959. Lens of Sutton Association.

21C136 as yet without WESTWARD HO nameplates in malachite green leaving Victoria station on a boat train in April 1947. Jim Flint and Jim Harbart, transporttreasury

34043 COMBE MARTIN at Bournemouth MPD in September 1955. The wedge-shaped cab was fitted at Eastleigh during a general overhaul in June 1952 and 4,500-gallon tender 3310 was modified at the same time, one of only three tenders so treated in the same year. Modification of the remaining tenders did not resume until 1957 with the beginning of the rebuilding programme. Worthy of note is the low position of the cab number and the lack of a black cab skirt. Bournemouth was one of those sheds closely observable from a platform end and almost everything was visible including the distinctive girder shelter to the lifting shop and the 20,000 gallon water softener beyond. John Eyers, courtesy South Western Circle.

34061 73 SQUADRON and 34009 LYME REGIS at Bournemouth shed in 1963, with the driver of 34009 oiling the rods and straps in preparation for the locomotive's return journey to Waterloo. There is a glimpse of Drummond M7 0-4-4T 30056 on the far right, and a rear view of another M7 standing on the centre road inside the shed. Canon Alec George, transporttreasury

BOURNEMOUTH

The shed at Bournemouth occupied a cramped raised area to the west of the station; it had its origins back in 1885 with the opening by the LSWR of the station on 20 July that year. There were two shed buildings, separated by a 50ft turntable and a coal platform. Proposals surfaced over the years to move to a more spacious site at Bournemouth West, or Branksome but these came to nought and the shed soldiered on with its cramped and awkward site to the end of steam. All that could be done was to extend three roads at the rear to afford some extra room. Improvements by the Southern in the 1930s (the sums expended on the Running Department in that decade alone must have been colossal, overall) included a new 50 ton hoist and a 65ft turntable, extra inspection pits in a rearranged yard, an electric crane for coaling with the old coaling platform demolished. A water softener was installed in 1938. British Railways provided a new asbestos roof on a steel framing.

Many light Pacifics and most of the Merchant Navys found themselves working from Bournemouth at one time or another. The old place closed with the end of steam in 1967 and looking at the cleared site since, it is difficult to imagine an important and busy engine shed ever stood there at all.

A Bournemouth engine since transfer from Nine Elms in June 1957, 35021 NEW ZEALAND LINE with tender 3342 (6,500 gallons) is at Dorchester South with the 9.42am Waterloo-Weymouth on 13 September 1958. The driver is sat looking back along the train awaiting the guard's 'right away' although with the 'boards' on, no movement can take place until the driver gets signal clearance. If the fireman has things right, he will have been running the fire down but keeping the steam pressure and boiler level up in preparation for the locomotive going on shed at Weymouth. It was all downhill from Dorchester Junction, so running down the bank through Bincombe tunnel to the station at Weymouth no firing will be needed, just keeping up the water level in the boiler. L.R. Freeman, transporttreasury

35002 UNION CASTLE rebuilt in May 1958 passing Vauxhall on 28 April 1962 with the 1.30pm Waterloo to Bournemouth. L.R. Freeman, transporttreasury

34028 EDDYSTONE (rebuilt August 1958) stands at Platform 1, Basingstoke with the 10.45am Waterloo to Bournemouth Central via Ringwood on 2 July 1961. John Eyers, courtesy South Western Circle.

Bournemouth's shed code 71B is clear on the smokebox door of 34037 CLOVELLY as the crew refill the tender at Nine Elms on 17 February 1962. John Eyers, courtesy South Western Circle.

Bournemouth West station on Sunday 31 March 1963 with 34042 DORCHESTER at the head of the 9.25am to Waterloo. John Eyers, courtesy South Western Circle.

Left. Bournemouth's 34045 OTTERY ST. MARY passes Wimbledon on a snowy day with the 10.8am Bournemouth West to Waterloo, 2 January 1962. John Eyers, courtesy South Western Circle.

Below. Hopefully, the steam heating is working properly in the carriages of the 11.12am Basingstoke to Waterloo passing Wimbledon hauled by Bournemouth's 34044 WOOLACOMBE the same day, 2 January 1962. In my experience as a fireman, if our locomotive was not steaming too well out on the road the first thing to be turned off, unfortunately for the passengers, would be the steam heating valve to conserve pressure in the boiler. We did get complaints (mainly from the guard) on the rare occasion this happened, but in true footplate fashion, we carried on regardless. Better the passengers got there than not. Anyway, we were warm! John Eyers, courtesy South Western Circle.

34110 66 SQUADRON arriving at Surbiton with the 8.50am from Bournemouth Central on 19 May 1957. It was the last in the class to enter traffic, on 26 January 1951, carrying a nameplate only, lacking plaque or crest. D.L. Bradley in his RCTS *Locomotives of the Southern Railway Part 2* reflects on this: *when 66 SQUADRON entered traffic in early 1951, the contractor providing badges could no longer do so, for the craftsman preparing them had retired and no replacement could be found. As a result, nameplates only were carried.* Lens of Sutton Association, John Faulkner Collection.

35003 ROYAL MAIL with steam escaping from the safety valves, at Waterloo with the 9.30am to Bournemouth on 15 August 1965. The fireman is coupling the engine to the train as the tail lamp is still in place on the bufferbeam after arriving light engine from Nine Elms and the correct disc code has yet to be put in place. L.R. Freeman, transporttreasury

With the mechanical coaling plant looming in the background, 34093 SAUNTON gets 'squared up' at Nine Elms in September 1965. The engine had gone to Eastleigh in September 1964, part of the move to get Pacifics out of the capital so as to ease maintenance. Ron Smith, transporttreasury

EASTLEIGH

Eastleigh engine shed opened in 1903, a vast structure with vaulting giant roof pitches, a slated roof and glazed end gables, in keeping with the style of LSWR building at the time. It enjoyed generous proportions with fifteen through roads plus a repair bay. A ramped coaling stage was provided with four roads leading to the turntable. There were more than a hundred locomotives on the books and inevitably the Southern carried out improvements during the 1930s, including a 20,000 gallon water softener and new offices. The latter were destroyed by enemy bombing in 1940, and the former dormitory underneath the large water tank adjacent to the coal stage was then converted as substitute accommodation. Eastleigh never had a larger turntable than the original 55ft example, and a triangle was eventually laid out for larger locomotives to turn. This was an extremely busy depot with plenty of work on the SR and ex-GWR lines both passenger and freight including the ocean liner traffic between Southampton and Waterloo.

Eastleigh did not have Merchant Navys though of course they were frequently to be found there. In fact the shed was not particularly notable for Pacifics at all. Only a handful worked from the shed in the 1950s and it was the 1960s before numbers of light Pacifics were based at Eastleigh; this was due to increasing numbers becoming available with, especially, electrification in the east and the later move to relieve Nine Elms of maintaining them – this had to do with staff problems, rather as Stratford parcelled out the maintenance of its Britannias to Norwich.

The photographer has caught the exact moment that the fireman hurls the fine ash from the blade of his shovel. 35020 BIBBY LINE, as already mentioned, was the Merchant Navy that famously suffered a crank axle failure, at Crewkerne, on 24 April 1953 leading to all the Bulleid Pacifics being temporarily withdrawn to be examined for similar defects. There was more to this scene than meets the eye – see next. A.E. West, courtesy Mike King.

Until the 1960s, when there were many more photographers and a rapidly shrinking number of subjects, photographers rarely thought to record the less glamorous side of steam locomotive work, when they required to be 'squared up' on the shed. With clinker thrown out from the firebox, ashpans raked out and the fine ash shovelled from smokeboxes swirling in the breeze, certainly this was it was something to avoid rather than stand around appreciating! So these three photographs at Eastleigh shed on 18 June 1949 are quite out of the ordinary, showing fireman W. Polman attending to 35020 BIBBY LINE, a Nine Elms engine which has contrived to turn up while working the Bournemouth Belle. Fireman Polman, armed with a firing shovel with which he will clear the char from the smokebox, is pleased to pose in front of 35020 in its malachite green livery, still retaining its Southern Railway smokebox door roundel. Worthy of note is the presence of a King Arthur 4-6-0 on the right. It is fitted with electric marker lights powered by a Stones generator, and a tubular ladder in the style carried on the tenders of the Bulleid Pacifics. A.E. West, courtesy Mike King.

While these photographs are certainly something out of the ordinary for their subject matter, they are noteworthy for an entirely different reason. The Nine Elms engine on the 'Belle' worked through, out and home on the 115 mile trip to Bournemouth West. For it to find itself at Eastleigh some sort of failure must have occurred, such to necessitate its removal from the train. Probably after the requisite attention it is being 'squared up' so it can be put on a train home. That it retained the headboard is interesting; either the cockney crew were reluctant to let it go or the rescue engine was unsuited to bear it – a bunker-first M7 maybe! (There were up and down pilots ready for such an event, but one or the other might have already been called to action.) The engine is 'head down' on what was termed the 'Big Engine' disposal pit avoiding road, laid out for the triangle. The extra-long smoke deflectors fitted to 35020 for the 1948 Locomotive Exchanges are seen to good effect as fireman Polman begins to shovel the smokebox stuff. Shovelling hot ash and cinders from the smokebox, especially in wind or, maybe worse, wind and rain, I hardly need assure readers, was a profoundly unenviable task. Despite all efforts it got everywhere, under your collar and down your neck. Heaps of clinker and ash stretch along the length of the locomotive and beyond. BIBBY LINE was prepared as the spare engine for the 1948 Locomotive Exchanges and as well as the extra length smoke deflectors got a modified cab, a Flaman Speed recorder and an LMS tender, the SR tenders lacking water scoops. 35020 did not take part in the Exchanges although it retained the LMS tender until June 1948. The Flaman Speed recorder can be seen attached to the rear driving wheel; BR number on the cab but retaining SOUTHERN on the tender. A Bulleid Q1 0-6-0 lurks in the background. A.E. West, courtesy Mike King.

34061 73 SQUADRON passing Woking with a down Rotterdam Lloyd boat train on 28 October 1961. John Eyers, courtesy South Western Circle.

Eastleigh on a Sunday in 1963. The depot had approximately 100-120 locomotives on its books and a staff of nearly 600 which included 184 pairs of drivers and firemen. At one time during the glory days of the Ocean Liner traffic before the Second World War, the depot had 24 sets of men principally for the trains from Southampton Docks. 'The boats' were all, of course, to a greater or lesser extent 'conditional' in that although a liner's departure was more or less fixed in advance, the arrival of any vessel could be delayed by adverse conditions – conversely, kinder weather in the Atlantic or a special effort demanded of the Captain might see a ship arrive early. Canon Alec George, transporttreasury

34004 YEOVIL during a break from duties in the yard at Clapham Junction on 9 June 1962. The engine is on 40 or 41 road, facing 'head up' (towards Waterloo) and adjacent to the down Windsor local line platform road 6. There were specific duties, for both Nine Elms and Feltham (mainly tank) engines, for the empty stock working into and out of Waterloo, to Clapham Junction carriage sidings. Main line engines too, were roped in, 'filling in' before returning down country. YEOVIL, pointing 'wrong way' for a return west and low on coal, would be one of those so engaged. The fireman, if it is he, looks in some despair. As a Yeovil Town fireman, this is one locomotive that I particularly wanted to work on; no such luck for, although an Exmouth Junction engine, it went to Bricklayers Arms after rebuilding. L.R. Freeman, transporttreasury

34016 BODMIN, rebuilt in April 1958, at Platform 15 at Waterloo station. The locomotive has been uncoupled from the train and a tail lamp placed on the buffer beam for the short journey to Nine Elms. A tail lamp is also in place on the rear coach with the driver and fireman looking out for the empty stock to be moved away before they and 34016 follow the train out to the platform end and embark on the run to Nine Elms. John Eyers, transporttreasury

34030 WATERSMEET in BR green with original cab, at Exmouth Junction on 22 August 1950. A stalwart at Exmouth Junction since the dawn of BR, it was withdrawn in September 1964. A.E. West, courtesy Mike King.

Exmouth Junction on 23 July 1958, solidly built in ferro-concrete under a northlight pattern roof with smoke chutes. It measured 270ft long by 235ft wide, with twelve roads each of which was 249ft long with inspection pits running the whole length of the building. There was an additional road under separate cover, walled off from the main depot, the Repair Shop which housed a travelling 50 ton crane, running the length of the building – hence the local name 'Lifting Hall'. The raised roof accommodated the crane. The large mechanical coaling plant had a capacity of 300 tons; with one exception this was the maximum employed in Britain and none of the dozens built pre-War exceeded this size. The exception was Nine Elms; at 400 tons it probably proved too liable to crush the coal in the bunkers and was not replicated. HMRS Collection.

EXMOUTH JUNCTION

The first shed building at Exmouth Junction had been an enormous barn of a structure fashioned, almost unbelievably, in corrugated iron and opened in 1887. This was a hostage to fortune by any measure and so it proved; it was in a parlous state within thirty years. The elements had taken their inexorable toll with sheets of rusty corrugated iron flapping and banging in the wind, rain coming through largely unhindered. Many of the windows had parted company with their frames. Work started in the summer of 1924, made more protracted by the need for locomotives to carry on using the old premises at the same time, which was not easy. An electrically operated 65ft turntable installed near the main line to the south of the new shed was the first part of the remodelling. The new shed building would have twelve roads plus a lifting shop and as parts of the new shed became usable so the old portions of the former premises were demolished. Seven roads were in use by May 1926, along with the coppersmiths and blacksmiths shops. A giant mechanical 300-ton coaling plant was erected to the south west corner near the main line. The new shed was mostly operational by 1927 although alterations were still being done to the repair shops in October 1929. When compete, the brand new shed at Exmouth Junction was the largest on the Southern Railway outside of the London area, built in the new technology of ferro-concrete under a northlight pattern roof. Along with its contemporary, Feltham, it was the most modern engine shed in the country. In my firing days during the late 1950s and early 1960s it was always an impressive place to visit, more so as here was the largest concentration of Bulleid Pacifics anywhere. It was the only shed that I worked to that had a District Motive Power Superintendent – in my day Mr A.W. Johnson. Exmouth Junction was responsible, until they eventually closed one by one, the sub-sheds at: Okehampton, Ilfracombe, Bude, Wadebridge, Barnstaple Junction, Exmouth, Sidmouth, Exmouth, Seaton, Callington, Launceston and Lyme Regis. At its peak, the shed had a staff of 430 which included some 120 crews. Incorporation into the Western Region in 1963 was like the tramp of doom. The grand old place closed to steam in June 1965 remaining open for a short term to service diesel locomotives, and the occasional steam locomotive which penetrated from Salisbury needing coal and water. It closed completely from 7 March 1967 with the shed buildings and the coal hopper demolished in 1970. Exmouth Junction had more Bulleid Pacifics on its books over time than any other depot; certainly most of the Merchant Navys spent time allocated there and probably this went for the light Pacifics too.

34004 YEOVIL in BR green with extended smoke deflectors, in the yard at Exmouth Junction on 1 October 1952. Fourth in the class, it was named at Yeovil Town station on 2 November 1945 by the Mayor, Councillor W.S. Vosper. The crest carries the County of Somerset coat of arms, 'Dragon rampant Gules holding in the claws a Mace erect Azure.' 34004 was one of three (34004, 34005, 34006) selected to take part in the Locomotive Exchanges in 1948. All three were ushered into Brighton Works in April for each to be fitted with wedge shaped cabs, Flaman speed recorders, inside ashpan dampers, extended smoke deflectors, improved mechanical lubricators. 34004 additionally required tablet exchange equipment for working over the single track Highland main line between Perth and Inverness. Each locomotive also had its drag boxes, drawgear and footplate altered to accept an LMS 4,000-gallon tender fitted with water pick up apparatus. L.R. Freeman, transporttreasury

With the high-roofed 'Lifting Hall' in the background, 34048 CREDITON is in faded malachite green at Exmouth Junction on 22 August 1950. A.E. West, courtesy Mike King.

21C105 not named as yet, in malachite green with small smoke deflectors alongside the up platform at Exeter Central on 28 August 1945. The tail lamp is on the tender indicating that the engine is moving forward on its way to Exmouth Junction shed. The lower quadrant signal in the foreground relates to the up through line and not to the up platform line that the engine is travelling on; the signal that the crew will be looking at is positioned at the end of the up platform. R.M. Casserley, courtesy M. Casserley.

Exeter prison looms beyond 21C110 (no name yet) in malachite green ready to leave Exeter Central station with an up train on 24 April 1946. The steam rising from the safety valves recalls one of the problems with the early light Pacifics which were provided with three safety valves ahead of the boiler dome. Upon braking, water would surge forward in the boiler ejecting the contents through the safety valves soaking anyone unlucky enough to be in range. Later modifications saw the safety valves reduced to two and repositioned further back along the boiler barrel. Lens of Sutton Association.

21C106 BUDE in the malachite green livery with yellow banding and the splendid Southern Railway roundel, at Exeter St. David's with a train from Ilfracombe. Lens of Sutton Association.

34014 BUDLEIGH SALTERTON arriving at Chapleton station with the 2.20pm Ilfracombe to Waterloo on 29 August 1956. Chapleton, between Barnstaple Junction and Yeoford, opened in 1875. The station building, immaculately restored, is now in private hands with Exeter-Barnstaple trains nowadays using the former down platform. Lens of Sutton Association, Denis Cullum Collection.

34080 74 SQUADRON passing Ashwater station with the 9.33am two-coach up ACE from Padstow on 6 March 1961. Upon arrival at Halwill Junction the train will combine with the Bude portion of the train. John Eyers, courtesy South Western Circle.

34081 92 SQUADRON with the 4.50pm Ilfracombe to Exeter Central at Barnstaple Junction on 2 September 1963. John Eyers, courtesy South Western Circle.

34060 25 SQUADRON with an up train at Barnstaple Junction in August 1956, E1R 0-6-2T 32608 shunting wagons in the bay platform. John Eyers, courtesy South Western Circle.

34016 BODMIN leaving Barnstaple Junction on 13 June 1956 with the 6.25am Yeovil Town to Ilfracombe. RailOnline

34015 EXMOUTH alongside the Barnstaple Junction coal stage; coal has been delivered from the simple mechanical hoist and the fireman is trimming the stuff in the tender. It was a routine task, one that I've done innumerable times. The coal bunker of M7 0-4-4T 30256 can be seen on the left and a N class 2-6-0 lurks in the background. John Eyers, courtesy South Western Circle.

34065 HURRICANE on 'Part 2' of the up Atlantic Coast Express at Barnstaple Junction on 7 September 1963. The engine shed suffered a fire late on leaving it in this skeletal state for its last few years. The wonder is it was not demolished straight away. John Eyers, courtesy South Western Circle.

34033 CHARD approaching Barnstaple Junction with the 7.45am Ilfracombe to Exeter Central in July 1956. I recall this engine on the Salisbury-Exeter main line as a good steamer, but we endured a blowback from the firebox on entering Crewkerne tunnel one day with an up stopper from Exeter Central. It was thoroughly alarming but with no serious injury – 'merely' singed eyebrows and slight burns to face and arms. This was regarded as fairly inconsequential back then! My hair was mercifully unscathed – see page 95... John Eyers, courtesy South Western Circle.

34069 HAWKINGE with the 4.21pm Exeter Central-Ilfracombe on the curving bridge over the River Taw. The wrought iron bridge of 7½ chains radius curved through 90 degrees which must have made it highly unusual if not unique in the country – certainly for a line operated by Pacifics at any rate! It was 213 yards long on seventeen spans consisting of fifteen pairs of main girders each with a length of forty feet. There was a 15mph speed restriction, effective throughout its length and in fact extended from Barnstaple Junction to Barnstaple Town stations. The bridge was dismantled in 1977. John Eyers, courtesy South Western Circle.

34070 MANSTON on 5 September 1963, approaching Pottington Crossing with the 5.57pm Ilfracombe to Barnstaple Junction. John Eyers, courtesy South Western Circle.

Left. 34078 222 SQUADRON casts a smoky pall around Ilfracombe station while waiting departure with the 12.15 to Waterloo, on 6 June 1963. John Eyers, courtesy South Western Circle.

Below. 34023 BLACKMORE VALE arriving at Ilfracombe on 18 May 1959 with the 6.25am from Yeovil Town. The first passenger train to depart from Yeovil Town station on weekday mornings, this was Exmouth Junction Duty No.523. Exmouth Junction men worked an up freight from Exmouth Junction sidings on Mondays to Fridays at 1.20am, changing engines at Yeovil Junction at 3.8am with the Exmouth Junction men, turning and watering the engine before proceeding light to Yeovil Town for coaling, then working the aforementioned 6.25am Yeovil Town to Ilfracombe. The Exmouth Junction men were relieved at Exeter Central. The 6.25am was worked by Yeovil men on Saturdays until the end of the summer service in 1964. Another through train to Ilfracombe left Yeovil Town on weekdays at 7.50am. Yeovil men worked this as far as Exeter Central. K.L. Cook, Rail Archive Stephenson.

There has been a crew changeover at Okehampton as 34062 17 SQUADRON waits for parcels to be unloaded from the leading brake on 25 May 1961. It will next take the train, the Plymouth portion of the 9am from Waterloo, on its way. The rebuilt light Pacifics were permitted between Exeter and Plymouth in 1960 but were never allowed to work over the North Devon and North Cornwall lines.
L.F. Freeman, transporttreasury

34023 BLACKMORE VALE entering Okehampton station with the down ACE on 25th May 1961; the battery box for the AWS system fitted in May 1960 can be seen above the bufferbeam. The coaling stage and part of the turntable can be seen in the background. L.R. Freeman, transporttreasury

34030 WATERSMEET arriving at Okehampton with a troop train from Tavistock on 27 May 1961. At one time the station had sidings west of the station for troop trains, military vehicles and equipment serving the nearby Okehampton Camp. The sidings proved useful for the motorail service from Surbiton between 1960 and 1964. L.R. Freeman, transporttreasury

34032 CAMELFORD arriving with the down ACE at Okehampton on 2 June 1960. L.R. Freeman, transporttreasury.

34065 HURRICANE at Okehampton with the 8.41am from Exeter Central on 1 June 1960. It had entered traffic as 21C164 in July 1947 and had been named at Waterloo station along with LORD BEAVERBROOK and SPITFIRE as mentioned earlier. L.R. Freeman, transporttreasury

The smoke vents of the little engine shed can be seen above the carriages behind 34072 257 SQUADRON at Okehampton with a down Plymouth train on 14 July 1959. 34072, new to traffic in April 1948, was one of the later series 34071-34090 that emerged from Brighton Works with the 9ft wide Vee cabs and larger 5,500 gallon tenders, although by the date of this photograph the tender had been swapped at Eastleigh for a 4,500 gallon version, in November 1957. R.C. Riley, transporttreasury

Top. Okehampton station stood majestically on the hillside 750ft above sea level, with the town laid out below. It opened on 3 October 1871 on East Hill, bordering Dartmoor to the south, with the town centre half a mile away. It became an important junction with the opening of the North Cornwall Railway and the line to Bude. Trains joined and divided here including the Atlantic Coast Express. Engine crews too. A pair of Exmouth Junction engines, 34017 ILFRACOMBE (rebuilt November 1957) and 34025 WHIMPLE (October 1957) await their next duty at Okehampton on 10 October 1953, stabled adjacent to the coaling stage and 70ft turntable installed in 1947 which enabled larger engines such as the S15s to work the Meldon Quarry ballast trains. R.E. Vincent, transporttreasury

Middle. On its long journey to London the 8.25am Plymouth-Waterloo stops at Okehampton behind 34107 BLANDFORD FORUM in BR green on 1 June 1960. Remarkably Okehampton station reopened to passengers on Saturday 20 November 2021, as part of the 'Dartmoor Line' the first line to be reinstated under the Department for Transport's 'Restoring your Railway' initiative. Trains run seven days a week between Okehampton, Crediton and Exeter St. David's providing for daily commuters, with most trains calling at Exeter Central (the best station for visiting the shops in the city centre). Latterly the service has become hourly. L.R. Freeman, transporttreasury

With 5½ miles to go to Padstow (259¾ miles from Waterloo) 34110 66 SQUADRON arrives at Wadebridge with the down ACE on 15 September 1960. Small Prairie 5564 is in the background, prior to running around its train before returning to Bodmin Road station. John Eyers, courtesy South Western Circle.

34069 HAWKINGE at Wadebridge on 8 June 1963, reversing to collect a single coach standing on the siding in the distance, to form the 6.13pm to Padstow. John Eyers, courtesy of South Western Circle.

34014 BUDLEIGH SALTERTON at Wadebridge in June 1955 awaits passage to the engine shed (over on the left, at the north side of the station). The impressive signal gantry, with its four upper quadrant signal arms controlled by the East box seen in the distance, will shortly allow its progress forward and reversal into the shed yard. The locomotive went new to Exmouth Junction as 21C114 in November 1945 and was named at Budleigh Salterton station on 26 June 1946; such occasions were seen by the Southern as useful publicity and PR (if we had such a term then) and the locals would turn out in force. The Mayor could be roped in or in the case of a Battle of Britain a senior local RAF Officer and the event would be reported, with photographs, in the local press. We should not underestimate either the profoundly positive impression these singularly-looking engines had on both the casual observer and the more initiated; Eric Youldon, late lamented of this parish, first saw one as a boy and never forgot it. So the system-wide namings were not off the cuff events, but a determined, planned strategy – which worked! R.E. Vincent, transporttreasury

34066 SPITFIRE, a Stewarts Lane locomotive until transferred to Exmouth Junction in February 1961, at Exeter St. David's with the down Padstow ACE on 5 May 1963. John Eyers, courtesy South Western Circle.

34011 TAVISTOCK with the down Ilfracombe portion of the ACE at Exeter St. David's on 5 September 1963. John Eyers, courtesy South Western Circle.

34023 BLACKMORE VALE with modified tender 3311 and the second BR emblem, arriving at Exeter Central with the up Plymouth ACE on 4 May 1964. The shunter is standing by the leading coach ready to uncouple the engine which will then proceed to Exmouth Junction MPD for turning, coal, and the rest. A Merchant Navy will be waiting ahead on the up main, to couple up to the train once 34023 is out of the way. Other coaches will be attached before proceeding to Waterloo. 80041 standing alongside the down platform on the left had arrived from Tonbridge, another Eastern refugee, in June 1962. This was a very busy station back in the day with many engine movements; passenger trains being split, reformed, restaurant cars, banking engines and so on. With so much going on, it was my favourite. Alec Swain, transporttreasury

Top. 34061 73 SQUADRON at Exeter Central with the up Padstow ACE on 4 May 1964; the fireman has already changed the headcode to the one denoting engines travelling to Exmouth Junction MPD. Alec Swain, transporttreasury.

Middle. 34062 17 SQUADRON in charge of an up stopper at Exeter Central on 23 August 1963. The train has a GWR 'Fruit D' together with three-set No.890, formed of two BR Mk.1s and a Bulleid. A.E. West, courtesy Mike King.

Below. 34034 HONITON, rebuilt in August 1960 and allocated to Exmouth Junction since its transfer from Plymouth Friary back in March 1952, awaits departure from Exeter Central with the 5.52pm to Waterloo on 4 September 1961. The rebuilds always looked impressive, superb engines to work on. Many is the time I have been on an one at this spot, a West Country, an S15 or 'Arthur' and very occasionally a 'Packet'. Unforgettable was the heat from the built-up fire, the noise and the aroma of steam, hot oil and smoke; with a touch on the steam blower to keep the fumes out of the cab, steam pressure high on the clock, awaiting the sound of the guard's whistle resounding along the platform, then pulling forward, slowly at first, with the engine getting into its stride to tackle the climb up through Blackboy tunnel past Exmouth Junction heading east. John Eyers, courtesy South Western Circle.

34011 TAVISTOCK entering Sidmouth Junction with the 1.10pm Exeter Central to Salisbury on 24 May 1961. The gate box (it had five levers for operating the level crossing gates) can be partly seen to the left of the locomotive. The gateman worked the levers in conjunction with the signalman in the main signal box which was positioned east of the station alongside the up siding and main line. The gates could not be opened until the locking was released by the signalman. L.R. Freeman, transporttreasury

After descending the eight mile 1 in 80 from Honiton tunnel and signalled for the up through line, Exmouth Junction's 35004 CUNARD WHITE STAR in blue with a modified cab approaches Seaton Junction with a goods train from Exmouth Junction sidings to Salisbury on 12 March 1952. That horizontal strengthening rib was characteristic of locomotives built using 'limpet board' for the casing. It can be seen running the length of the casing above the nameplate. If an engine was not steaming well on the journey from Exeter, there was a very good chance to rally the boiler round when running down the eight mile bank to Seaton Junction. It happened to me one day with an old 'Arthur' working an up stopper from Exeter Central, and by the time we had reached the bottom of the bank we had more than enough steam. A.E. West, courtesy Mike King.

34055 FIGHTER PILOT with an Exeter Central-Salisbury stopping train at Seaton Junction at 1.50pm on 12 March 1952, in the days when there were nineteen stations open between Salisbury and Exeter Central. This is the type of train, passenger or goods, that we Yeovil Town crews worked along the Salisbury-Exeter main line; not for us the hectic pace of express trains, we had a more sedate life, although not without its highlights at times! There were only two stations between Salisbury and Exeter Central that had through roads enabling faster trains to overtake the slower services – Yeovil Junction and here at Seaton Junction where on summer Saturdays a procession of expresses heading east or west would accelerate through. A certain number of stopping trains were booked to wait here for a comparatively long length of time. During the summer of 1958 for instance the 10.37am and the 1.8pm up trains from Exeter Central were booked to wait for 13 and 11 minutes respectively, while the 12.56pm from Salisbury waited for a miserable 34 minutes. Often on busy summer Saturdays a signalling inspector would be in the box to make quick decisions on holding late running trains on the local lines thus enabling faster and more important trains to overtake them. A.E. West, courtesy Mike King.

With the tender not yet displaying the new BR ownership, although there is a smokebox numberplate, the pioneer West Country 34001 EXETER is near Crewkerne Tunnel with a Waterloo-Exeter Central service on 16 April 1949. The locomotive is in malachite with the three yellow horizontal bands along the casing and tender. Longer standard smoke deflectors have been fitted, complete with the 'strake' at the top of the deflector for mounting the Devon Belle boards. The engine was named in an official ceremony at Exeter Central station on 10 July 1945; it was not the first of the class to be named, that accolade belonged to 21C102 SALISBURY named on the previous day 9 July. A.E. West, courtesy Mike King.

34024 TAMAR VALLEY leaving Seaton Junction with a stopping service for Exeter Central on 12 March 1952. The vehicle at the rear is an ancient LSWR Bullion Van (SPECIE) used for years to take gold bullion and other precious stuff carried on the ocean liners. They probably hadn't borne anything much in the way of valuables for some time and were reclassified in the early 1950s as simple luggage vans – though presumably they'd certainly be harder to break in to than most! The plume of steam in the distance is coming from Drummond M7 0-4-4T 30045 working the Seaton branch train. Leaving this station with a westbound train, this is where a fireman had to be on the ball, for ahead is the eight mile ascent to Honiton tunnel mostly at a gradient of 1 in 80. All fireman have laboured up this bank in weather fair or foul and in daylight and darkness and I was ever pleased to see the distant signal for Honiton Incline box appearing ahead. It couldn't be more welcome, for it meant that we were nearing the summit and at the end of the worst part of the climb from Seaton Junction. Entering the 1,345 yard tunnel, the longest on the Southern Region, the glow from the firebox reflected eerily around the cab and danced against the tunnel wall; sparks

from the chimney would rebound off the tunnel roof and bounce on the cab roof. Half way through the tunnel the gradient changed and we started running downhill, the driver easing back the regulator and the reverser. A.E. West, courtesy Mike King.

34033 CHARD leaving Seaton Junction for the east with milk on 24 September 1964. The place was a major centre for the traffic from the Express Dairy creamery which adjoined the west end of the up platform. I have fired 34033 on a number of occasions, and have already touched upon an alarming blowback experienced with it – see page 82. It happened with driver Garth Ostler on an up stopper from Exeter Central when coasting through Crewkerne Tunnel. Although the steam blower was turned on and the regulator closed in preparation to stop at Crewkerne station, the locomotive, with the weight of our train, was freewheeling down the incline. I had the fire door closed but that didn't stop a jet of flame coming into the cab; there were no serious injuries apart from a slight burn to my face, and the hair on my arms and eyebrows singed. It was with singular good fortune that I had my grease top cap on, otherwise my Elvis Presley quiff may have suffered irreparable damage! Garth escaped unscathed, as he had his head stuck out of the window looking out for the signals for Crewkerne Gates. Milk

traffic was quite pronounced on the Salisbury-Exeter line with tanks despatched from the Express Dairy creamery at Seaton Junction to London, and also from the former United Dairies milk processing plants at Chard Junction and Semley (United Dairies amalgamated with Cow & Gate in 1959 becoming Unigate). More loaded tank wagons would be tripped to Templecombe for onward despatch to London from Bailey Gate and Bason Bridge on the Somerset & Dorset line, where they would be formed into complete trains or attached to up passenger services, all balanced with long rakes of empties returning to the West. Loaded tanks were also attached to stopping passenger trains from the West and tripped to Templecombe; we used to work an up stopper from Exeter Central which was booked to collect two or three daily from Chard Junction and take them to Templecombe. A.E. West, courtesy Mike King.

35024 was the first Merchant Navy to appear in the blue livery with red lining, in February 1949. A while later, in March, this was amended with black and white lining. Here it is with covered nameplates and 6,000 gallon tender 3346 near Crewkerne tunnel on 16 April 1949. It was formally named EAST ASIATIC COMPANY by HRH Prince Axel of Denmark, the chairman of the shipping company, on 5 May 1949 at Waterloo station. The plates were not to be revealed until the ceremony but it was inconvenient – impossible in fact – to fit them 'on the day' for it involved a fair bit of work. Given the high profile of the companies involved it was deemed politic to keep the plates hidden and it must have been one of the Eastleigh carpenters' more unconventional jobs to make the covers up. All this wasn't usually necessary with the light Pacifics; some were covered certainly but a few weren't, and entered service without any ceremony at all. For the Battle of Britains there might be nowhere close that could practically serve as a suitable location, while some Squadrons in particular were disbanded or were stationed elsewhere in the Kingdom – or even abroad. 35004 was repainted in BR green in June 1951, the first of the class so treated. By way of aside, the climb towards Crewkerne tunnel from Crewkerne station for down trains is a severe one at 1 in 80 culminating at the west end of the 206 yard tunnel. Plodding up the bank with a heavy goods train bound for Exmouth Junction sidings we would be almost at walking pace, every part of the engine alive and pulsating with power. The regulator would be wide open and the reverser fully forward as the dark gaping mouth of the tunnel appeared ahead. There was no need to attend to the fire as there'd be ample in the box. We'd enter the tunnel with a loud warning blast on the whistle. The rest is clamour, smoke and sparks, lighting up the roof and sides of the tunnel, the noise indescribable. The exhaust beat suddenly softens as we exit from the tunnel and climb the last few yards before running down the bank to Chard Junction, regulator and reverser now eased back and the injector on. A.E. West, courtesy Mike King.

Top. 34072 257 SQUADRON comes through Sutton Bingham, a sleepy wayside station west of Yeovil Junction, heading the 12.5pm Waterloo-Ilfracombe on 2 September 1961. It had been reduced to an unstaffed Halt in August the previous year. For Exeter-bound trains passing through Sutton Bingham there followed a welcome long downhill stretch curving to the right passing Sutton Bingham reservoir. It was a good part of the line to catch up a bit of time and get a move on. With a down goods not booked to stop at Crewkerne I'd have the injector trimmed and working, keeping the firebox packed full in the back corners and under the door, all in preparation for the three mile climb ahead from Hardington to Crewkerne tunnel. John Eyers, courtesy South Western Circle.

Middle. With the 'boards' at danger 34074 46 SQUADRON is at Yeovil Junction with the 11.10am Plymouth to Brighton on 23 June 1963, taking water on the up platform while the fireman is pulling coal forward. This elegant six arm signal gantry was the largest on the main line between Salisbury and Exeter Central. On a gantry such as this the signals are read by a footplate crew from left to right, the height of an arm on its post indicating its importance with regard to the route it refers to. The upper quadrant arms, from left to right are: up bay to Yeovil Town branch, bay to up main, up main to Yeovil Town branch, up main, up through to Yeovil Town branch, up through. On the far right of the gantry is the rear of the Sykes banner repeater which relates to the down through starting signal at the west end of the station. The fireman will have the firebox already crammed full in readiness for the daunting ascent from Sherborne to Milborne Port. John Eyers, courtesy South Western Circle.

Bottom. A pair of Bulleid Pacifics at Yeovil Junction on 21 March 1964, 34083 605 SQUADRON on the left near the shunters' cabin and on the right 34107 BLANDFORD FORUM. The latter, having arrived in the up bay as a light engine, tender-first from Yeovil Town, is signalled on to the up main, and pulling forward to travel only as far as Yeovil Junction 'A' box. There, it will stand on the up main line to await the arrival of the 1.10pm Exeter Central-Salisbury which it will work onwards, with the engine from Exeter travelling to Yeovil Town for servicing.

34092 CITY OF WELLS stands alongside the bay platform at Yeovil Junction with the 4.6pm Yeovil Town-Salisbury on 2 September 1961. The engine, having brought the train from Yeovil Town station tender-first, has run round and now faces smokebox forward for the journey to Salisbury. These will be Salisbury men who had worked down to Yeovil Junction earlier on Salisbury Duty No.479 with a class 4 BR Standard 2-6-0 on the 11.4am stopper from Salisbury. Upon arrival at Yeovil Junction the engine was uncoupled from the train, turned and watered and left behind the down platform with a few wagons and a guards van to form the pick-up goods worked by Yeovil Town men to Crewkerne, Chard Junction and Axminster, and return to Yeovil Junction. The Salisbury crew would then prepare their engine in Yeovil Town shed to work the 4.6pm stopper to Salisbury. John Eyers, courtesy South Western Circle.

Salisbury's 34099 LYNMOUTH awaiting signal clearance at Yeovil Junction on 23 March 1963. It is waiting to take the branch to Yeovil Town for servicing at the MPD. There is a train already signalled from the branch platform to Yeovil Town; this is probably the push & pull shuttle that plied between the two stations meeting the main line stopping services. 34099 will have to wait its turn to be signalled along the branch. John Eyers courtesy South Western Circle.

34013 OKEHAMPTON on the No.1 shed road at Yeovil Town. The coaling platform on the left was in use until the end of the Second World War when (we could have done with it earlier!) a steam crane arrived complete with six tubs making coaling a lot easier than hand shovelling from wagons – though we still had to shovel the stuff into the tubs worked by the crane. The roof for the coaling stage was provided in 1920 'at a cost of £176 plus £6.10 shillings for lighting'; astonishingly here it is nearly forty years later, albeit with a few holes. This of course was my home shed where I spent many happy days as a cleaner and a fireman. 34013 has arrived from Yeovil Junction for 'squaring up' and is standing on one of two roads served by the steam crane. Most engines carried approximately five tons and arrived on shed almost empty; during busy times the coalmen were always pleased to have a helping hand in loading the coal tubs. Engine cleaners did more than their job title would suggest; sweeping out the drivers cabin for instance, a thankless job done on a daily basis. Fag ash, old newspapers and food scraps everywhere on the tables, all of which had to be cleaned off and wiped down and the cabin brushed out. The best job was cycling round the town delivering 'alterations' – traffic notices – for the next day to off duty drivers and fireman. I have helped out with all the shed 'trades' at times, replacing firebars in fireboxes, passing new fire bricks through the firedoor, taking away the old bricks in a wheelbarrow and tipping them at the rear of the shed. The fitters too were always pleased to have a hand especially with heavy stuff, changing brake blocks or springs and of course there was always the chance to assist a fireman with squaring up an engine newly arrived on shed. That is how I learnt to master the long handled clinker shovel, digging it into the firebox and gingerly with gloved hands withdrawing the clinker shovel from the box, swinging it around the cab and throwing the hot clinker down on to the ground. Happy days indeed.

34061 73 SQUADRON with a cut-down modified tender and a slightly crumpled casing stands in the shed yard (Yeovil Town signal box in the background) on 18 April 1964. At the risk of repeating myself, the Bulleids in my estimation could not be bettered. They were a 'fireman's engine', free steaming with a spacious, comfortable and relatively draught free cab (the BR Standard classes 4 and 5 were dreadful in this respect) with a good turn of speed when needed. Drawbacks included a propensity to slip, although certain drivers seemed able to avoid this entirely. This has all been mentioned in the text but an awkward feature was the sand boxes on the air smooth engines which required a ladder to reach them. Yeovil Town did not have an allocation of Bulleid locomotives, although we had many duties using them between Salisbury and Exeter Central. RCTS Collection.

Top. With tail lamp on the bufferbeam and fresh off shed, 34065 HURRICANE awaits the platform starting signal at Yeovil Town station to clear before proceeding tender first to Yeovil Junction on 28 July 1963. I have done this many times, with all classes of engine; with the turntable up on the main line at Yeovil Junction and the shed some distance away at Town, there were innumerable light engine movements over 24 hours between the two. In a comfortable enclosed cab like this it could be a pleasure but on an S15 4-6-0 on a very wet dark early winter morning with the waterproof sheet up between the cab and the tender not so much. Worthy of note on the front of the engine is the Exmouth Junction shed plate 72A, the conduit connecting the electric marker lights, and the battery box for the AWS above the buffer beam with the 'bash' plate for the system itself positioned behind the coupling. We had about 100 men at Yeovil Town, sharing a convivial friendly atmosphere. Yeovil then was a small market town, we all knew each other and I'd gone to school with many of my engine cleaner comrades including Vic Rigden, Dave Turner, Alan Rogers and Frank Randall all of whom were a year older than I. My late younger brother Nigel, and our cousin Pete Stevens were also firemen there. At one time we had our own football team 'Railway United' and a skittle team that played in the 'Alexandra' (known locally as the Alex) pub opposite the Town station. If ever a job and a place to work was almost 100% perfect then this was it. I have many fond memories of life at the shed, of so many steam locomotives and of the men I once worked with, their ranks now sadly thinned. Mike King Collection.

Left. Looking from the station footbridge at Yeovil Town on 19 August 1962, 34098 TEMPLECOMBE awaiting departure with the 4.6pm to Salisbury. This train was worked by Salisbury men and upon arrival at Yeovil Junction the engine will run around the train and depart smokebox first to Salisbury. H.B. Priestley, transporttreasury.

Exmouth Junction's 35005 CANADIAN PACIFIC arriving at Templecombe on 23 August 1952 with the empty milk tanks from Clapham Junction. Some of the empty tanks will be left here for onward despatch to the Unigate milk processing plants at Bailey Gate and Bason Bridge on the Somerset & Dorset line, while others will be left at Chard Junction and Seaton Junction. The running in board on the platform at this once important rail interchange station in Somerset, displays the following information for rail passengers: TEMPLECOMBE CHANGE FOR SOMERSET & DORSET LINE BOURNEMOUTH BATH BRISTOL BIRMINGHAM & THE NORTH. Templecombe was unique in the heart of rural Somerset where Southern Railway locomotives could be seen in the Upper yard alongside older locomotives of the LMS/Midland and I well remember more than once sitting in the cab of a West Country in the Upper yard waiting to enter the station with the empty stock of the 12.42pm Templecombe-Salisbury stopper. Alongside might be the unaccustomed sight of a 4F 0-6-0 with the stock, say, for the 12pm for Bath Green Park. R.E. Toop.

34023 BLACKMORE VALE at Templecombe Platform 2 with the 8.51am Exeter Central-Salisbury on 26 March 1953. There is a long non-taxing descent from Templecombe for the crew of 34023 coming up, followed by a climb of 1 in 100 through the 742 yard Buckhorn Weston tunnel. This could be a tricky place for footplate crews working an up train; there was a natural spring above the bore and in wet weather water cascaded down; in dry spells it merely dripped and trickled. The rails were seldom dry and if an engine was going to slip, then you could bet your boots it would happen here! On rare occasions even one of the sure-footed S15 4-6-0s slipped here. Once through the tunnel and breasting the rise there are two miles down hill to Gillingham station whence there follows a sharp ascent to Semley. John Eyers courtesy South Western Circle.

A westbound train is in the far distance as long-term Exmouth Junction resident 35003 ROYAL MAIL in BR green tackles the Semley bank between Gillingham and Semley with the Padstow 1st portion of the up Atlantic Coast Express on 21 August 1958. For crews, working trains up from Exeter Central, as described earlier, this was the last serious ascent before reaching Salisbury, starting from the platform end at Gillingham. Hugh Ballantyne.

35023 HOLLAND-AFRIKA LINE climbs the Semley bank with the second (Torrington) portion of the up ACE on 21 August 1958. 35023 never received blue livery being the last of the class to retain malachite green until repainted BR green in March 1952. The Exmouth Junction fireman, gazing at the photographer has everything under control; he will have the firebox crammed full and the injector steaming against the boiler on a magnificent engine such as this one. The permanent way gang standing on the down main line also seem to be interested in the photographer. By some oversight there are two separate duty numbers displayed on the head code discs. Hugh Ballantyne.

After tackling the climb from Tisbury 34058 **SIR FREDERICK PILE** runs past Semley with the 11.30am Brighton-Plymouth on 18 September 1962. Semley was the summit of the line for eastbound and westbound trains running between Gillingham and Tisbury and for either crew there would be a 'breather', a chance to rally an engine round if not doing so good for steam while coasting on the relevant downhill sections. John Eyers, courtesy South Western Circle.

34065 HURRICANE passing Wilton South with an up goods on 18 September 1962. The station was well known as the changeover point for engines on the Devon Belle when it was running, 1947-54. The fresh engine for the down service would wait on the siding on the left for its counterpart to arrive with the train from Waterloo. Arriving at this station with an up stopper, my driver and I would be preparing to 'bail out' upon arrival at Salisbury, the eastern limit of our working. If the engine was coming off and going to the shed for squaring up, I would have been running the fire down, at the same time keeping the steam level up. If the engine was working through, we would change over on the platform and it was a matter of pride to hand the engine over with a full firebox, plenty of steam, coal pulled forward on the tender, the cab floor swept clean with the hand brush and washed down with the pep pipe – in the same manner as I would expect to receive an engine from another crew. John Eyers, courtesy South Western Circle.

Malachite 21C2 UNION CASTLE arriving at Salisbury from Exeter; it is an undated view, though the clues are there. The engine acquired malachite green (from wartime black) in July 1946 and in January 1950 lost its gun metal plates on tender and cab. Part of the GWR engine shed can be seen on the far right and the Southern Railway locomotive shed is in the left distance. The GWR signal on the right, controlled by the GWR 'C' signal box, refers to trains leaving the station for the Westbury line and is nothing to do with the Southern main line. Salisbury West box is in the background. Jim Flint and Jim Harbart.

34062 17 SQUADRON departs from Salisbury on Exmouth Junction Duty No.526, the 10.30am Exeter Central to Waterloo, in October 1959.

The pioneer 35001 CHANNEL PACKET at Basingstoke in 1954 in BR green with black and orange lining, applied at Eastleigh Works in May 1952 in place of the blue livery. transporttreasury

34036 WESTWARD HO pauses at Woking with the 5pm Waterloo-Yeovil Town on 11 August 1962. This is the engine that fellow Yeovil Town fireman Dave Brown recalls in his memories, a rough trip with driver Fred Symonds while working an empty stock train from Salisbury to Yeovil Junction on 17 December 1964. John Eyres, courtesy South Western Circle.

Exmouth Junction locomotives worked the empty milk tanks back to the West of England, like 35008 ORIENT LINE with the 3.54pm Clapham Junction-Exmouth Junction on 3 August 1956. As with the Meldon Quarry ballast empties, more than one rake would be combined, as seen here. Lens of Sutton Association, Denis Cullum Collection.

34032 CAMELFORD rebuilt in October the previous year, running past Wimbledon with the down milk empties on 29 March 1961. John Eyers, courtesy South Western Circle.

Exmouth Junction's 35024 EAST ASIATIC COMPANY at Nine Elms in 1954. Two versions of clinker shovels short and long handled (there was a longer one used on S15s etc) have been placed against the cab by the fireman who presumably is making the fire up ready to go on the road. The tools were kept in tunnels in the tender. transporttreasury

35005 CANADIAN PACIFIC on the turntable at Nine Elms on 10 September 1949. It had been fitted with a Berkley mechanical stoker in April 1948 and subsequent trials were conducted between Waterloo and Exeter. While such stokers made sense on giant American locomotives, for instance, they weren't of any special utility in British conditions. The Berkley stoker was removed in April 1951 and 35003 reallocated to Exmouth Junction. A.E. West, courtesy Mike King.

NINE ELMS

The progenitor of the principal locomotive depot of the LSWR was a seven road through shed positioned near to the works alongside the main line opened about the time of the extension to Waterloo in 1848. It could have been the biggest and best equipped shed in the Kingdom, with a pair of coaling stages and 40ft turntables at either end. Further improvements involved the site of the early shed disappearing under running lines and its replacement by a semi-roundhouse set at right angles to the main line. This new building had twenty-six roads radiating from two 42ft turntables; two large, covered coal stages were provided alongside the approach roads. The later depot came into use c.1889 when a large brick single ended building under a pitched slated roof with fifteen roads came into use, positioned to the west of the roundhouse. It measured 365ft by 235ft with all fifteen roads leading on to a new 50ft turntable, a large new coal stage supported on brick arches was also provided. When another building was put up alongside, this would become known as the 'Old Shed.' This eleven-road extension was authorised in 1910; it was similarly built in brick although the roof pitches and central vents were transverse to those of the original building. It inevitably became known as the 'New Shed'. The LSWR in its last months of existence decided to replace the coaling stage with a 400-ton mechanical plant in ferro-concrete, though it did not come into use until after the grouping. Under the Southern Railway the depot ranked second only to Stewarts Lane in locomotive allocation on the entire system.

Extensive bomb damage occurred during the Second World War; the whole area suffered greatly in fact and a number of streets round about no longer served houses but empty, cleared ground, after the war's end.

As for the Pacifics allocated it would be quicker to list those *not* allocated!

34094 MORTEHOE is at Platform 4 at Brockenhurst on 31 June 1961, with the 12.40pm Eastleigh-Bournemouth via Ringwood. John Eyers, courtesy South Western Circle.

Standing amid the accumulated heaps of clinker and ash at Nine Elms on 31 August 1946, 21C13 BLUE FUNNEL is in wartime black. It had come to Nine Elms in February 1945 and was named later that year, on 17 April, at Waterloo station. R.C. Riley, transporttreasury

34090 SIR EUSTACE MISSENDEN SOUTHERN RAILWAY in front of the 'New Shed' at Nine Elms on 25 May 1963; alongside is 73065. Ron Smith, transporttreasury

35015 ROTTERDAM LLOYD and 35014 NEDERLAND LINE at Nine Elms on 5 July 1951. The tender of 35015 has had the raves at the top removed, whereas the tender on 35014 is in original condition; also worthy of note is the central rib running the length of the casing on 35014 and the differing styles of the ladder tops on the tenders. To the right is the 'New Shed' and the engines are standing on roads that were once *inside* the 'Old Shed'. Bomb damage was such that the roof had to be very largely cut back, as can be appreciated here. There never was a need post-war for the accommodation to be restored and indeed so vast was the site at Nine Elms that much of it was frequently under-occupied. Eric Sawford, transporttreasury

35011 GENERAL STEAM NAVIGATION in malachite green, at Nine Elms on 5 July 1951. It had been renumbered from 21C11 in November 1948 with BRITISH RAILWAYS on the tender, at a time when the emblems had yet to be determined. The engine has been coaled and the fireman up aloft will be making sure none of this generous provision is liable to fall off. Nine Elms was a bit out of the ordinary in that it lay quite a way below the main lines and very much out of the ordinary in that the buildings and yard were at right angles to the running lines. Not only that, engines had to reverse off a spur to get into the place. 35011 has come from Waterloo tender first (of course) and has been turned (the table is over to the right). It will leave like this, smokebox first and reverse on to the main line, so heading for Waterloo tender first – the 'right way round' to take out its next train. Eric Sawford, transporttreasury

Top. 35017 BELGIAN MARINE absolutely gleaming in ex-works condition on the coaling road at Nine Elms upon return from Eastleigh Works repainted from malachite into BR blue in July 1949. 35017 participated in the 1948 Locomotive Exchanges, fitted with LMS tender 10123 working trains between Kings Cross-Leeds and Euston-Carlisle. J.C. Flemons, transporttreasury

Middle. 21C20 BIBBY LINE in grubby malachite green with original cab, at Nine Elms in July 1947. Selected as the spare engine for the 1948 Locomotive Exchanges and modified accordingly, its services were in the event not required, although it ran with LMS tender 10373 on the Southern Region until June 1948. R.E. Vincent, transporttreasury

Bottom. 35018 BRITISH INDIA LINE at Nine Elms in 1956. It had been the first rebuild to appear, a few months previously, revealed to the public at Eastleigh on 9 February the first of the class to be so treated. It was shortly afterwards sent to Waterloo for inspection by the Board. Unfortunately after a couple of weeks it suffered a problematic radius rod at Farnborough and had to be hauled dead to Eastleigh. transporttreasury

Yet-to-be named 21C159 in malachite green livery, in company with a Drummond M7 0-4-4T and 0-8-0T 949 HECATE, at Nine Elms in July 1947. It had been allocated here since April of the same year and was named SIR ARCHIBALD SINCLAIR by the man himself, one of the great unsung heroes of the Battle of Britain, at Waterloo station on 24 February 1948. R.E. Vincent, transporttreasury

34008 PADSTOW at Nine Elms on 9 October 1954. It had gone new to Exmouth Junction as 21C108 in September 1945 and transferred to Nine Elms in April 1951. L.R. Freeman, transporttreasury

Left. The penultimate Merchant Navy, 35029 **ELLERMAN LINES**, waiting to depart Waterloo with the Bournemouth Belle on 28 April 1962. The AWS protector plate has been fitted behind the coupling, although the battery box has not yet been fixed. With thousands of locomotives being equipped across BR, such an 'interim' condition was quite common as parts sometimes got scarce. The cable of the Smiths speedometer which the locomotive was fitted with in June 1961 can be seen attached to the rear driving wheel. J. Harrold, transporttreasury

Below. 34012 LAUNCESTON approaching Surbiton on 24 April 1955 with the 10.54am Waterloo-Bournemouth Central diverted via East Putney. Lens of Sutton Association

Left. At the end of the day the country will resound with the chimes of Big Ben, celebrations, revellers making merry, fireworks and refrains of *Auld Lang Syne* at the stroke of midnight as 35019 FRENCH LINE C.G.T. passes Clapham Junction with the down Bournemouth Belle on New Year's Eve 1960. L. Nicholson, transporttreasury

Below. One of the Nine Elms 'Packets', 35016 ELDERS FYFFES in blue livery running through Seaton Junction on the down through line with the ACE on 12 March 1952. The crew are lucky as they have a crack at the eight-mile Honiton Incline mostly at a grade of 1 in 80. A.E. West, courtesy Mike King.

Left. 34006 BUDE passing Tulse Hill signal box on 27 May 1956. It retains the extra length smoke deflectors fitted for the 1948 Locomotive Exchanges. R.C. Riley, transporttreasury

Below. 34071 601 SQUADRON at the head of the 9.0am Waterloo to the West of England on 23 March 1963. John Eyers, courtesy South Western Circle.

35001 CHANNEL PACKET at the west end of the down platform at Yeovil Junction with the 9.0am Waterloo to the West of England on 30 September 1961. The 9.0am from Waterloo was worked as part of Nine Elms Duty No.5, booked for a Merchant Navy equipped with a large tender. 35001 will work back to Waterloo later in the day with the 4.30pm from Exeter Central. L.R. Freeman, transport treasury

34006 BUDE at Bournemouth Central on 24 April 1962, turned and all ready to work home to Waterloo. In the background are Bournemouth's 34053 SIR KEITH PARK and Eastleigh's Q 0-6-0 30542. Lens of Sutton Association.

34007 WADEBRIDGE in BR green approaching Wimbledon off the East Putney line with a London Midland Region theatrical special to Southampton on 31 March 1957. Lens of Sutton Association.

34031 TORRINGTON at Bournemouth Central with the 1.30pm Waterloo to Weymouth on Sunday 29 March 1964. There has been a crew changeover by the look of it, as the engineman standing by the cab has his bag slung over his shoulder, a tea can dangling from his right hand. John Eyers, courtesy South Western Circle.

34007 WADEBRIDGE arriving at Templecombe with the 12.45pm Torrington to Waterloo on 14 September 1957. Part of the extensive Upper yard lies over on the right. During my footplate days, the freight traffic dealt with here was very heavy with trains arriving and departing at all hours. There was considerable exchange traffic to and from the Midlands on the Somerset & Dorset line via Bath. We Yeovil men used to shunt in the Upper yard at night usually with a Yeovil U 2-6-0 which had arrived at Templecombe earlier in the day on the 4.54pm Salisbury-Templecombe (Yeovil Duty 513, worked by Salisbury men). We would arrive at about 1am after riding on the footplate of an up freight train, and swap with another Yeovil crew. The shunting at night was never ending with just a ten or fifteen minute break when the shunters stopped for a cup of tea and a bite to eat. We would return home working the 5.30am Templecombe-Yeovil Junction freight; upon arrival at Yeovil Junction we would reverse our train into the down sidings, then at 6.20am depart light engine tender-first to Sherborne and shunt the yard until it was time to change over with the crew of the 5am Salisbury-Yeovil Town booked to arrive at 7.28am. This we would work after reversal at Yeovil Junction to the Town station where we would be relieved on the platform by another Yeovil crew. They would continue shunting with the train and take the engine to shed for squaring up etc. We'd wander over to the cabin and after washing off the worst of the coal dust I'd set off for home on my bicycle to see mum for breakfast. All would be well with the world. Lens of Sutton Association.

34010 SIDMOUTH passing Esher on 19 March 1955 with the 10.30am Waterloo to Weymouth. Lens of Sutton Association.

Above. 34017 ILFRACOMBE at Basingstoke with the 10.54am Waterloo to Bournemouth Central on 22 July 1962. Some joker has chalked 'claped out' (*sic!*) on the protective screen over the vacuum cylinders on top of the tender, obviously not referring to the steaming qualities of the engine as the safety valves are in full flow, and the fireman has a full firebox from the volume of smoke issuing from the chimney. John Eyers, courtesy South Western Circle.

Left. 34093 SAUNTON passing Esher with the 9am from Waterloo to the West of England on 28 October 1961. John Eyers, courtesy South Western Circle.

34007 WADEBRIDGE at Eastleigh with the 12.35pm (SO) Waterloo to Weymouth on 4 February 1961. L.R. Freeman, transporttreasury

With the original Southern Railway style BOURNEMOUTH BELLE headboard 34061 73 SQUADRON runs past Lymington Junction with the all-Pullman down 'Belle' on 29 May 1950. The Lymington branch runs in the immediate foreground. The receiving post for the single line token is on the right with an adjacent exquisite gas lamp; the neat sleeper foot crossing for the signalman leads to a small wooden platform and the 'cow's horn' setting down post on the left. Lymington Junction signal box closed in April 1967. J. C. Flemons, transporttreasury

Rebuilt since 1959 and on Nine Elms books since April 1951, 34010 SIDMOUTH passes Winchfield on 16 May 1964 with the 11am Bournemouth to Waterloo. Lens of Sutton Association.

34012 LAUNCESTON with the 10.14 Waterloo to Bournemouth at Wimbledon West Junction on 19 April 1957. Lens of Sutton Association.

Right. 35014 NEDERLAND LINE of Nine Elms, having worked the down ACE from Waterloo, occupies one of the pits at Exmouth Junction on 22 August 1950. I always enjoyed working to Exeter Central and bringing our engine to Exmouth Junction to be squared up as we did not have time in our duty to do it ourselves. Of course, we did not work on a train with the prestige of the ACE; ours would have been a stopper which we had brought down from Yeovil Junction as part of a through service from Salisbury. After leaving our engine we would walk across to the shed office and get the number of the engine we were working back home. On certain duties, we would swap with an incoming crew on a passenger train on the up platform at Exeter Central if the engine was working through. In that case we would get a lift on an engine that would be travelling light engine to the station. A.E. West, courtesy Mike King.

Below. 35019 FRENCH LINE C.G.T. in BR blue at Exmouth Junction on 22 August 1950. The engine is reversing to the turntable, passing one of the Junction's S15 4-6-0s 30847, another superb class of engine that I worked on as a young fireman; good steaming locomotives, very strong, we worked them on passenger and goods trains. A.E. West, courtesy of Mike King.

Above. 35019 FRENCH LINE C.G.T. now on the 70ft turntable installed in 1947 in replacement for a 65ft unit, ready for the run back to Waterloo on 22 August 1950. The engine had worked the Royal train to Sherborne a few months previously, on 1 June. It had taken part in the 1948 Locomotive Exchanges working between Kings Cross and Leeds for two days before suffering firebox defects – a brick arch failure presumably. After restoration it worked between Paddington and Plymouth. A.E. West, courtesy Mike King.

Left. After its brief sojourn on trial on the Eastern Region at Stratford between April and May 1949, 34059 SIR ARCHIBALD SINCLAIR in malachite green is in charge of a down Bournemouth train at Winchester on 5 August 1949. A.E. West, courtesy Mike King.

Left. Malachite green 34059 SIR ARCHIBALD SINCLAIR coming off the turntable at Nine Elms, in the period after renumbering to 34059 in March 1949 but before repainting to BR green in April 1951. Jim Flint and Jim Harbart, transporttreasury

Below. 34101 HARTLAND at Waterloo station on 31 May 1964 with the 10.30am to Bournemouth and Weymouth. It is the only preserved example of an Eastleigh-built Bulleid light Pacific (there were after all only six of them). John Eyers, courtesy South Western Circle.

34006 BUDE passing Surbiton on 27 May 1956 with a troop train from Southampton Docks to Waterloo via Alton. Lens of Sutton Association.

35014 NEDERLAND LINE approaching Vauxhall with the up Bournemouth Belle on 6 June 1953. It was repainted from malachite green into BR green in August 1951 and never got the blue. L.R. Freeman, transporttreasury

35012 UNITED STATES LINES in BR green with THE ROYAL WESSEX headboard up, at Nine Elms on 9 October 1954. The train was inaugurated on 3 May 1951 to mark the Festival of Britain of that year. The up service departed from Weymouth at 7.34am and the down left Waterloo at 4.35pm. For the initial train on 3 May 1951 Bournemouth's 34105 SWANAGE worked the up train, and 34008 PADSTOW (Nine Elms) was at the head of the down train of thirteen coaches. Portions went hither and thither, reminiscent somewhat of the ACE. Six coaches for Bournemouth West were detached at Bournemouth Central, with five for Weymouth and two for Swanage detached at Wareham. For the up service, the Swanage and Bournemouth West sections would be waiting in advance on a siding at Bournemouth Central and were attached to the rear of the up train upon arrival from Weymouth. The Bournemouth West portion ran for the last time on 4 September 1965 when the station closed. With the onset of electrification and the two-hour services to and from Bournemouth, 8 July 1967 was the final day for the Royal Wessex. L.R. Freeman, transporttreasury

Plymouth Friary in BR days. The gable glazing, blown out in the air raids of the Second World War, has been replaced by corrugated sheeting. One of the four B4 0-4-0Ts for dock work is standing on the right stabled between an ancient LSWR coach which has seen better days and a Drummond M7 0-4-4T. Friary was also responsible for the sub-shed at Callington which housed the former PD&SWJR 0-6-2Ts.

Exmouth Junction's 34109 SIR TRAFFORD LEIGH MALLORY leaves Plymouth Friary station on 20 August 1958 with only a few weeks to go before the station closed to passenger traffic, on 15 September. Friary shed had lost its four light Pacifics the previous year at the end of the summer timetable. Standing alongside at the bay platform, attached to a train of Southern Region stock with its WR headlamps displaying the code for the Southern Region main line via Okehampton, is Churchward 2-6-0 7333 with a stopping service to Exeter Central. For route familiarisation, some WR services were operated by SR crews and vice versa, in the event of one main line or the other being blocked. Typically the WR might suffer storm damage at Dawlish and the SR blizzards near Dartmoor. Of note is the ex-LSWR 'gate' coach in the foreground. A.E. Bennett, transporttreasury

PLYMOUTH FRIARY

Plymouth Friary shed opened in 1908 replacing a two road building nearer the station. The new three road shed was sited south of the line near Lucas Terrace Halt, first stop on the Turnchapel branch from Friary station. A handful of light Pacifics were allocated between 1948 and 1957 for the work (mainly) to Exeter and the shed's principal working, the Plymouth-Brightons. On weekdays the engine worked through to Salisbury, however, on Saturdays it worked throughout on the six-hour 200-mile trip to Brighton, the longest continuous run on the Southern Region. Its Bulleids, 34035, 34036, 34037 and 34038, were lost to Exmouth Junction in the autumn of 1957 and that shed afterwards provided the engine for the daily Plymouth to Brighton service. The turntable at Plymouth Friary was too small for the larger locomotives which turned instead via Mount Gould Junction and Cattewater Junction. Friary closed in May 1963.

Top. A Friary light Pacific since transfer from Exmouth Junction in April 1948, 34013 OKEHAMPTON newly painted in BR green, tackles the ascent from Templecombe with a down express on 13 May 1950. 34013 found itself back at Exmouth Junction in May 1951. The cattle wagons in the background are standing in the Upper yard. John Eyres, courtesy South Western Circle.

Bottom. 34036 WESTWARD HO (at Friary from 1950 to 1958) with a down train at Axminster station on 12 March 1952. One of the locomotives selected for the short-lived oil burning scheme, it was fitted with the 'Laidlaw Drew' equipment in February 1948, but reconverted to coal burning in November 1949. A.E. West, courtesy Mike King.

129

Salisbury on 20 September 1947, the final months of the Southern Railway. This view is exactly as I remember when I went on loan as an engine cleaner from Yeovil Town and later as a fireman, with engines lined up on the pit on the right, waiting to be squared up, coaled and watered, the line coming off the turntable and the many engines standing outside awaiting preparation or the next duty. What the photograph is unable to get across is the roar of safety valves lifting, the whistling of engines as they leave the shed for the station and the general noise of everyday life in a shed – plus the air would be heavy with steam and smoke. H.C. Casserley, courtesy M. Casserley.

Magnificently oily and begrimed, 34003 PLYMOUTH stands outside the shed on 18 February 1962 awaiting its next duty. 34054 LORD BEAVERBROOK can be glimpsed in the background. Crews of engines waiting to leave the shed had to strain their ears against the clamour for the call on the loud speaker system, clearing them to leave the yard. The message would come as the train that they would be working; '8.41 to Yeovil' etc. With a blast on the whistle we would move tender first towards the exit with the pointsman standing by his hut waving us out, and the ground signals 'off' guiding us along the route. In our case (returning to Yeovil) we'd be signalled either towards the station if working a passenger train or into the West yard backing on to a goods train or a rake of empty ballast wagons destined for Meldon Quarry. Tony Cousins, transporttreasury

SALISBURY

Rebuilding of Salisbury station at the turn of the century involved the demolition of the original shed buildings. A large modern depot on a spacious site to the west was erected by way of replacement. It opened in December 1901, built in brick under a slated roof of five pitches ten roads. A huge 100,000 gallon water tank surmounted a brick built dormitory adjacent to a 55ft turntable and there was a large elevated wooden coal stage from which engines could be coaled from either side. A 65ft turntable replaced the 55ft table in 1912, a 70ft turntable was installed in 1956. The nearby ex-GWR shed on the opposite side of the main line closed in November 1950 (although engines were stabled there for a time) with the Western Region engines subsequently being serviced at the Southern Region shed. Salisbury closed in July 1967 with the end of Southern steam; it became infamous as a storage yard for withdrawn steam locomotives from all over the Region before they were hauled off for scrap in South Wales.

Top. 34054 LORD BEAVERBROOK at the shed on 18 February 1962. I cannot fail but be impressed with the size of the lumps of coal on the tender. I would be more than happy to prepare the fire on a Bulleid with coal like that; if a mite oversize to go through the firedoor, a quick bash with the coal pick would do the trick to crack the lump and shovel it. Tony Cousins, transporttreasury

Bottom. 34009 LYME REGIS on 18 April 1964. One of the superb rebuilt light Pacifics, turned, coaled, watered with safety valves lifting, all prepared to return to Waterloo and its home shed at Nine Elms. Alec Swain, transporttreasury

With the starting signal at danger, 34014 BUDLEIGH SALTERTON stands at the west end of Salisbury station with the 1pm Waterloo to Plymouth on 8 August 1964. Assisting with coaling and watering of locomotives on up and down services between Waterloo and Exeter was common practice at Salisbury during the busy summer months. I describe this in my loan to Salisbury, doing exactly this, though I don't recall it being quite as precipitous as it clearly was! As soon as a train arrived, the crew changed over, while we young lads clambered up on the tender like monkeys to put the water bag in, then furiously shovel coal forward until the six-minute station stop was over and the train departed, almost at the moment we stepped off. Lens of Sutton Association.

34013 OKEHAMPTON in the down bay at Salisbury station on 18 April 1964 attached to Set 781 forming the 3.5pm to Exeter Central. Alec Swain, transporttreasury

34067 TANGMERE passing Weybridge with the 10.15am Waterloo to Ilfracombe and Torrington on 11 August 1962. My late brother Nigel and I worked on 34067 during our firing days on the Salisbury-Exeter main line and like most of the class it was a good free steaming 'fireman's engine'. About ten years ago the engine visited Yeovil Junction on a steam special and I was invited on to the footplate. As soon as I entered the cab and felt the heat from the firebox and looking at the gauges pipes and controls all the memories came flooding back. It was an emotional experience and, I must admit, there was a tear in my eye when I climbed down from the cab. I last fired one of these wonderful locomotives in service in July 1964 just before I left the railway. John Eyers, courtesy South Western Circle.

A sign of the times with track lifted from the down bay in the foreground at Grateley station, albeit leaving the wooden sleepers in situ for a later collection. 34014 BUDLEIGH SALTERTON pauses with the 6pm from Waterloo in 1964 before proceeding onwards to Salisbury. Grateley was the junction for the branch line to Amesbury opened 1902, closed to passenger traffic 1952, lingering on for goods traffic until 1963, the tracks of which can be seen in the background. Amesbury station was advertised by the LSWR as the 'closest station to Stonehenge.' The driver is looking back along the train awaiting the wave of the green flag and a blast on the whistle from the guard. Once the train is on the move it is the fireman's duty to keep a look back just in case a late arriving passenger running to catch the train might slip and fall between the platform and the moving train. Lens of Sutton Association.

34049 ANTI-AIRCRAFT COMMAND passing Andover Junction with an up goods on 29 March 1961. The problem with smoke and steam beating down and obscuring vision was never completely solved on the air-smooth locomotives, and various modified versions of the cowling were tried as seen here on 34049 with a Mk.1 modified version fitted by Eastleigh in March 1960. Not yielding the desired success the modified cowling was later removed. John Eyers, courtesy South Western Circle.

34052 LORD DOWDING passing Wimbledon and cracking on with the 11.45am Waterloo to Exmouth on 5 August 1961. John Eyers, courtesy South Western Circle.

35006 PENINSULAR & ORIENTAL S.N. Co., a Salisbury engine all its working life, at Exmouth Junction on 5 September 1958. Ron Smith, transporttreasury

One of Salisbury's Merchant Navys, 35004 CUNARD WHITE STAR approaching Crewkerne tunnel on 16 April 1949 with an excursion for Seaton, formed of LSWR non-corridor stock. It is in 'interim' state; BR number painted above the buffer beam in Southern Railway style, SR roundel on the smokebox door, BRITISH RAILWAYS on the tender. A.E. West, courtesy Mike King.

35006 PENINSULAR & ORIENTAL S.N.Co. in blue livery near Crewkerne with a down train on 26 March 1952. A.E. West, courtesy of Mike King.

34009 SHAW SAVILL passing Seaton Junction with Waterloo train on 12 March 1952.

34067 TANGMERE, a Salisbury engine since transfer from Stewarts Lane in May 1961, on the turntable at Nine Elms. Jim Flint and Jim Harbart, transporttreasury

Malachite 35010 BLUE STAR in another 'interim' style; SOUTHERN and its new number in the 'sunshine' style, at Nine Elms 10 September 1949. A.E. West, courtesy Mike King.

35026 LAMPORT & HOLT LINE, a Weymouth engine since transfer from Nine Elms in September 1964, on the GW 65ft over-girder turntable at Weymouth shed on 14 September 1966. I was not impressed with the turntables at the ex-GWR sheds such as here and at Westbury, both of which were manually operated and could be 'beasts' if the engine was not balanced perfectly. The turntables I have used, at Salisbury, Yeovil Junction and Exmouth Junction were much more modern and vacuum operated, using the system off the locomotive to power a traction motor which revolved the turntable. All this of course, involved by comparison almost no physical effort. RailOnline

WEYMOUTH

From earliest times the standard gauge LSWR and the broad gauge GWR maintained engine sheds at Weymouth. The broad gauge was abandoned in June 1874 and a decade later the GWR opened a modern four road shed to the north of the station. The small, cramped (and decrepit too, you suspect) original LSWR two road shed soldiered on even into Southern days but closed in January 1939 as the ground was required for station improvements. Engines were afterwards quartered at the GWR shed. The depot was transferred from the Western to the Southern Region in February 1958 when the shed code was altered from 82F to 71G changing to 70G September 1963. Although Bulleid Pacifics were daily visitors to Weymouth from other sheds, they were not allocated until 1964, by which time the place had acquired a distinct Southern 'look' with SR engines very much in the ascendency. Weymouth closed to steam on 9 July 1967 and like Salisbury became a storage point for withdrawn steam locomotives.

Bournemouth's 35008 ORIENT LINE on 27 August 1963. Having worked down with the 10.30am passenger service from Waterloo, the engine has been turned, coaled and watered in readiness to work the 5.30pm back to London. RailOnline

Bournemouth's 34084 253 SQUADRON takes water at Weymouth shed on 11 August 1963 before reversing on to the turntable in the background. Modified tender 3309 was attached to the locomotive during an overhaul at Eastleigh in April 1960 following the locomotive's involvement in the peculiar Hither Green accident of 20 February 1960. Working a Dover to Bricklayers Arms goods train, while moving out of the loop at Hither Green without a signal, it moved slowly through the stop blocks and toppled down the embankment. Cascading hot coals set fire to the cladding requiring the attendance of the local Fire Brigade. The firemen tore off the air-smooth casing to reveal the boiler beneath. RailOnline

The full sidings beyond are an indication of the once-prolific mail, parcel and goods traffic including fresh produce from the Channel Islands once handled at Weymouth. 34048 CREDITON is standing stationary on the engine departure line from Weymouth shed, ready to proceed to the station. The driver and fireman are watching the signal gantry for entry to the station. The fireman has already telephoned the signalman from the lineside box, giving the destination of the working; for example, I would let him know we were '7.30pm excursion to Yeovil' which would be acknowledged by the signalman. When ready, the route indicator on the gantry would display the platform number, with our waiting coaches. In those days, the route indicator could direct an engine into any one of the six platforms which Weymouth station had at the time. RailOnline

Arriving at Weymouth with an excursion train on 7 July 1963, the driver of Salisbury's 34059 SIR ARCHIBALD SINCLAIR seems interested in Hymek D7047 standing on the Weymouth shed departure line. The diesels had been around for a couple of years or more and, more probably, he simply knows the driver. The first regular diesel locomotive workings on the old GWR line between Bristol and Weymouth occurred as early as 16 September 1961 with Hymeks on the 10.10am SO Bristol-Weymouth, returning with the 3.25pm to Bristol. Diesel Multiple Units had started working services on the former GWR route from 6 April 1959, starting with a total of three up and three down workings per day interspersed with steam workings. Eventually of course the diesels replaced all the steam locomotives and fuelling points were provided at Westbury and Weymouth. RailOnline

34094 MORTEHOE, from Nine Elms and fresh off shed, is reversing along Platform 3 at Weymouth to couple on to the stock at the far end to form the 5.35pm to Waterloo on 1 August 1963. The middle sidings and the engine loop are on the left. Ron Smith, transporttreasury

35012 UNITED STATES LINES at Platform 3 at Weymouth on 7 September 1965 with the 5.30pm to Waterloo. An unwieldy parcel is being manoeuvred into the van – imagine attempting this on a Hitachi Class 800 in 2022. It was important for a fireman when leaving Weymouth to have a hot bright fire for a crack at the bank which extended almost from the end of the platform to the far end of Bincombe tunnel. I had a rebuilt Bulleid one Sunday on an evening return excursion to Yeovil with driver Harold 'Hammer' Ham; we passed Upwey Junction under clear signals and were well into the bank. Harold had the regulator wide open with our engine chopping off the beats in fine style as I tended the needs of the firebox, keeping the boiler level up with the injector singing away. We were now slowing as we neared the steepest part of the bank with, ahead of us, the first and shortest (at 56 yards) of the two tunnels we have to blast our way through. Bincombe Tunnel signal box up distant was off and, invitingly in front of us, the gaping dark mouth of the 814 yard Bincombe Tunnel, smoke and steam billowing out from the passage of a previous train. We ploughed on and with a warning blast on the whistle, entered the tunnel. The sound of our exhaust would rise to a deafening crescendo within the close confines of the tunnel. Harold had the steam sanding turned on just in case of a slip. Conditions in any tunnel are rarely less than unbearable but Bincombe was one of the worst with clouds of steam and smoke swirling around the cab making breathing difficult. The clamour in the tunnel would have been so loud that it would be difficult to know if we were moving or just slipping, so the best you could do was lean out of the cab and carefully touch the tunnel wall with the firing shovel. At last daylight would appear and we'd burst out into the fresh air – free! A moment to refresh our lungs before passing Bincombe Tunnel signal box and the banking engine siding. Although banking assistance was available from Weymouth I cannot recall any driver from Yeovil Town ever requesting one. A point of honour! Topping the bank it was time to ease the regulator and wind back the reverser as we neared Dorchester Junction. L.R. Freeman, transporttreasury

Templecombe's 4F 0-6-0 44146 and 34040 CREWKERNE depart from Bath Green Park with the 7.45am (SO) Bradford to Bournemouth in 1951. The Whitaker Tablet Apparatus on 34040 is already extended to collect the single-line tablet at Bath Junction for the section from there to Midford. transporttreasury

34043 COMBE MARTIN and 34044 WOOLACOMBE on down and up expresses respectively at Evercreech Junction on 6 July 1959. R.C. Riley, transporttreasury

BATH GREEN PARK

Although motive power on the Somerset & Dorset at Bath Green Park was the responsibility of the London Midland Region which had many locomotives on loan there, the S&D sheds were transferred to the Southern Region in February 1950. The result was that Bath (including the sub-shed at Radstock), Templecombe and Highbridge were recoded 71G, 71H and 71J respectively. As a probable replacement for the Stanier Black Five 4-6-0s, a light Pacific, Bournemouth's 34109 SIR TRAFFORD LEIGH MALLORY, less than one year old, was fitted with the S&D tablet exchange equipment on the tender and made a series of trial runs between Bournemouth and Bath in March 1951. The trials began with the seven coach semi-fast services to Bristol, concluding with the unaided ten-coach 'Pines Express' to and from Bournemouth. D. Bradley and David Milton in their book *Somerset and Dorset Locomotive History* (David & Charles) record that this 'proved to be almost too much for the engine and although the tests were considered officially satisfactory the load limit was set at 270 tons unaided over the Mendips. Their nominal increase in power over the Class 5s was offset by their lack of adhesion.'

Despite this, 34040, 34041, 34042 and 34043 were allocated to Bath Green Park for the summer of 1951 with more being borrowed from Bournemouth on summer Saturdays. Control of the motive power on the S&D was handed over to the Western Region in 1958 with the sheds renumbered into the '82' series with Bath (including sub-sheds at Radstock and Highbridge) becoming 82F and Templecombe 82G. Although no more Pacifics were allocated to Bath after 1954 they were daily visitors to the line including the final Saturday 5 March 1966 when 34006 and 34057 double-headed the LCGB. 'Somerset & Dorset' Rail Tour.

40564 and 34041 WILTON with the 10.35am (SO) Bournemouth to Manchester at Shepton Mallet Charlton Road on 20 August 1960. L.R. Freeman, transporttreasury

ON THE GREAT EASTERN

There was seen in some quarters to be an over-abundance of Pacifics on the Southern Region and the possibility arose of fifteen being transferred to the Great Eastern section of the Eastern Region. The ex-LNER Pacifics were barred from Liverpool Street and the lines out of there, leaving the express services to the Thompson B1 and B2 4-6-0s and the Gresley B17 4-6-0s. 34059 SIR ARCHIBALD SINCLAIR was sent on loan from Nine Elms to Stratford on 27 April 1949, at first working an empty stock train from Stratford to Norwich on 2 May and later in the month working the Norfolkman to Norwich and services to Parkeston Quay. 34059 was returned to the Southern Region in May 1949 and that would appear to be that. Certainly Stratford, with its perennial labour shortages, would have looked askance at the Bulleid gear. The idea was revived, however and 34039 was sent to Stratford on 8 May 1951 followed shortly afterwards by 34057 and 34065. The engines worked on the Liverpool Street to Cambridge services, and later the Norfolkman and the Continental services to Parkeston Quay. The temporary withdrawal due to a mechanical defect of the Britannia Pacifics from 22 October 1951 led to an engine crisis on the Eastern Region, partly filled by the loan in November 1951 of two more Bulleids, 34076 and 34089 from Ramsgate and Stewarts Lane. Upon the reinstatement of the Britannias the notion of using more Bulleids fizzled out and all were returned to the Southern.

Opposite. Alongside a B12 4-6-0 at Liverpool Street station, 34059 SIR ARCHIBALD SINCLAIR waits to leave with the Norfolkman express to Norwich in May 1949. J.C. Flemons, transporttreasury.

Top. Shock of the new. 34059 SIR ARCHIBALD SINCLAIR awaiting departure from Liverpool Street station with the 'Norfolkman' in May 1949 attracts attention. J.C. Flemons, transporttreasury

Left. 34039 BOSCASTLE under the control of driver Holliday departs tender-first from Haughley station on the Great Eastern main line between Liverpool Street station and Norwich with a Bury St. Edmunds to Ipswich stopping service in 1952. Dr Ian C. Allen, transporttreasury

145

EASTLEIGH WORKS

Exmouth Junction's 34027 TAW VALLEY with coupling rods removed at Eastleigh on 17 May 1953 awaiting entry to the Works for a general overhaul and the fitting of a wedge-shaped cab. Locomotives awaiting overhaul had to have the tender emptied of coal and water, and the boiler drained. L.R. Freeman, transporttreasury

35010 BLUE STAR in blue on 29 March 1951, in line for a general overhaul 6 April-12 May before return to its home shed at Nine Elms. 35010 had been fitted with a wedge-shaped cab and repainted from malachite green into BR blue in November 1949. L.R. Freeman, transporttreasury

34104 BERE ALSTON undergoing rebuilding at Eastleigh in April 1961. As noted, it was the last to be rebuilt, 13 March-13 May 1961.

Above. Awaiting the finishing touches after its rebuilding 35026 LAMPORT & HOLT LINE inside the Works on 9 February 1957 alongside a 2-6-4T. Two of the Derby-built Fairburn 2-6-4Ts from the LMR were tried out on all three sections of the Southern Region in 1948; the success of these trials led the SR to build a batch of them, 42066-42106, at Brighton between October 1950 and June 1951. The cabs of two more of the 2-6-4Ts lie on the floor. L.R. Freeman, transporttreasury

Left. 35017 BELGIAN MARINE in the works on 25 February 1961 undergoing a light intermediate overhaul between over February-April 1961. It returned afterwards to its home shed at Nine Elms where it had been resident since April 1945. Nick Nicholson, transporttreasury

The new main frames for 35004 CUNARD WHITE STAR set up inside Eastleigh Works on 21 June 1958 prior to its rebuilding. The large holes are drilled out to aid weight reduction. The locomotive was in the works between May-June 1958 before returning to Salisbury. Alec Swain, transporttreasury.

Exmouth Junction's 34079 141 SQUADRON inside Eastleigh Works stripped down for a light intermediate overhaul August-September 1960 surrounded by the paraphernalia of a busy railway workshop; coupling rods in the foreground, heavy lifting slings used by the overhead lifting crane strewn on the iron bench, chains and pipework dotted about, the only thing that is not replicated is the noise of hammering and banging, drilling, grinding, shouting, plus the aroma of metal work and welding. Roy Hobbs, transporttreasury

Ramsgate's 34098 TEMPLECOMBE ex-works in front of the main offices at Eastleigh on 8 November 1955 after undergoing a general overhaul. Eric Sawford, transporttreasury

34108 WINCANTON newly rebuilt at Eastleigh on 30 April 1961. Two remarkable contrasts beyond are USA 0-6-0T 30074 and an E5000 electric. James Harrold, transporttreasury

...05 (BARNSTAPLE) under construction in Brighton Works. It commenced building the first light Pacifics in mid-December ... with 21C101-21C120 released to traffic between May and December 1945. All the West Country and Battle of Britains ... built there except, as already related, 34095, 34097, 34099, 34101, 34102 and 34104 which were assigned to Eastleigh. ... were renumbered 34001-34070 after the formation of British Railways. 21C164 FIGHTER COMMAND ... engine to be built at Brighton, entering traffic in July 1947.

... under construction at Brighton; released to traffic 30 June 1945, it went to Exmouth Junction, staying there ... located to Bricklayers Arms. One hundred and ten light Pacifics were built which, with the thirty ... the Southern replete with 4-6-2s – when steam-worked passenger mileage is taken into account ... provision made even on the LNER. But of course they were, as a result of Bulleid's legerdemain, ... carried the names of cities, towns and geographical locations in the West Country and forty-four bore ... aircraft, airfields and so on associated with the Battle of Britain. The two exceptions were 34049 ... ND, an army unit under the direct control of Fighter Command and 34090 SIR EUSTACE MISSENDEN

21C128 (EDDYSTONE) under construction at Brighton Works in 1946.

Nothing like finishing on a strange sight. 21C133 (CHARD) is in three shades of works grey with white n~~~~
wonders) on the cab at Brighton on 21 June 1946. This confection has a way to go to match the tender~~~~
painted at Ashford Works) in malachite green with yellow bands. Wilfred Beckerlegge, Rail Archive S~~~~